Praise for the book

'This is the first book of its kind that I've read all the way through. I am a truck driver. My life is spent on highways, without a fixed address. Getting my hands on the book wasn't easy, I had to arrange to have it delivered to a friend's address. The book travels with me everywhere and I tell others of it.'—**Balulal Khandela**, truck driver, Laxmipura, Bhilwara

'A searing, painfully honest memoir of a Dalit's disenchantment with the RSS after serving it faithfully for years. Written in fluent and lucid prose, this is a compelling narrative of faith and betrayal, nationalism and casteism, fear and hope. Bhanwar Meghwanshi lays bare, from the inside, the strengths and the limitations of the RSS' formidable organisation and the dangers posed by its ideological project to turn India into a Hindu Rashtra. A must-read for all those concerned with the current direction of our politics and its implications for the country.'—**Shashi Tharoor**, M.P., and author of *Why I am a Hindu*

'Meghwanshi's bewilderment at the conspiracy of silence by the entire RSS organisation towards his efforts to challenge their practice of untouchability is painful to witness. As Meghwanshi recounts his Ambedkarite turn and his fight against the RSS, his story becomes a social document for the times.'—**Cynthia Stephen**, writer

'*I Could Not Be Hindu* is necessary reading in these days when dictatorial fascist tendencies have consumed the Indian psyche. It will open your eyes, free your thoughts and help you realise what authentic freedom is.'—**Benyamin**, author of *Goat Days*

'The game is up for the RSS. Now the scales will fall from the eyes of those members of the Dalit and backward communities who persist in mistaking the exploiter for a nurturer, predator for protector, cowardice for valour, and enmity for friendship... This book will go some way towards breaking the spell of religion.'—**Karmveer Shastri**, activist for rationalism, New Delhi

'The book teaches how, living in this murderous age, we may yet preserve ourselves from the menace that is the RSS.'—**Dr Naveen Joshi**, teacher of science, Almora, Uttarakhand

'A warning to Dalits not to be taken in by the two-faced RSS, with its blandishments about a pan-Hindu brotherhood and social cohesion.'—**Vinod Kumar Ashramiya**, Baran, Rajasthan

'This remarkable book by a remarkable man teaches the reader lessons for a life lived in service of the struggle for equality. It is as moving as informative.'—**Christophe Jaffrelot**, author of *The Hindu Nationalist Movement and Indian Politics*

'Paints a vivid picture of the organisational structure of the RSS, its ideology, schemes and designs, along with its narrow outlook and utterly evil intent towards the Bahujan and minority communities.'—**Jeevan Dagla**, former administrative official

'The book does not pull its punches as it challenges mindsets and reveals, with the unimpeachable dignity, how a rowdy karsevak was transformed into a committed humanist, a servant to the cause of love.'—**Ramesh Pataliya**, Palanpur, Gujarat

'A manual on how to escape the RSS' duplicity. Every social activist must read it. You will gain a new vision.'—**Dr Tara Ram Gautam**, intellectual

'The plain truth about the RSS, revealed with a unique combination of fact, reason and true-to-life narration. A most inspiring, absorbing story.'—**Govind Mayee**, a Dalit youth

'This book has changed the landscape of Dalit autobiography. Defiance is sharpened on the whetstone of ideas, as Bhanwar Meghwanshi transports us from plaintive suffering to rebellion, and from rebellion to new modes of thought.'—**Himanshu Pandya**, principal, Raniwada College, Jalore, Rajasthan

'You feel with the writer at every turn. If you are a Dalit, you know his humiliations well.'—**Samyak Nayak**, a Dalit youth

'I read this book in one go and it was a revelation. Meghwanshi's insider account of the RSS exposes Hindu nationalism for what it is—a desperate effort by the upper castes to retain their grip on the rest of society.'—**Jean Drèze**, intellectual and economist

'Every page alerts us to the fraud that is the Sangh; may it succeed in showing leftover sevaks their way out.'—**Brijmohan Nayak**

'A must-read for the Sangh's supporters and its opponents. Read this and be informed. Read it because it bears pain and agitation, and makes a jolting departure from sedated life. You'll see distraction, wandering, struggle and victory here.'—**Naresh Gurjar**, student leader, Bhilwara, Rajasthan

'I recommend it to every member of the Sangh.'—**Avinash Vikas Sharma**, a vigilant citizen, Kothiyan, Bhilwara, Rajasthan

'The feelings Omprakash Valmiki's *Joothan* left me with were revived by Bhanwar Meghwanshi's autobiography. It is the expression of truth, not merely as something experienced but *undergone*.'—**Dr Satyanarayan Satya**, children's writer

'This should be prescribed reading for all those youngsters with revanchist dreams of an Akhand Hindu Rashtra, especially those who come from deprived sections of society. An authoritative account of the web spun by the RSS, and a map showing the way out.'—**Samrat Baudh**, young writer, Gwalior, Madhya Pradesh

'Bhanwar walks into the secret caves of enemies and comes out alive. This book offers a roadmap to navigate a life of politics, caste and ideological differences. A memoir like this is nothing short of a miracle.'—**Perumal Murugan**, writer

I Could Not Be Hindu: The Story of a Dalit in the RSS

First published in English in hardback, 2020
This paperback edition, 2022
ISBN 9788194865490

First published in Hindi as *Mein ek karsevak tha by Navarun*, 2019
The Hindi text has been substantially expanded and revised

Navayana Publishing Pvt Ltd
155 2nd Floor
Shahpur Jat, New Delhi 110049
Phone: +91-11-26494795
navayana.org

Typeset by Inosoft Systems in Dante
Maps on pages 8–10 by Saumya Sethia

Printed by Sanjiv Palliwal, New Delhi

Distributed in South Asia by HarperCollins India
Subscribe to updates at navayana.org/subscribe
Follow on facebook.com/Navayana

I Could Not Be

I Could Not Be Hindu

The Story of a Dalit in the RSS

BHANWAR MEGHWANSHI

Translated from the Hindi by

Nivedita Menon

Mapping Bhanwar Meghwanshi's life

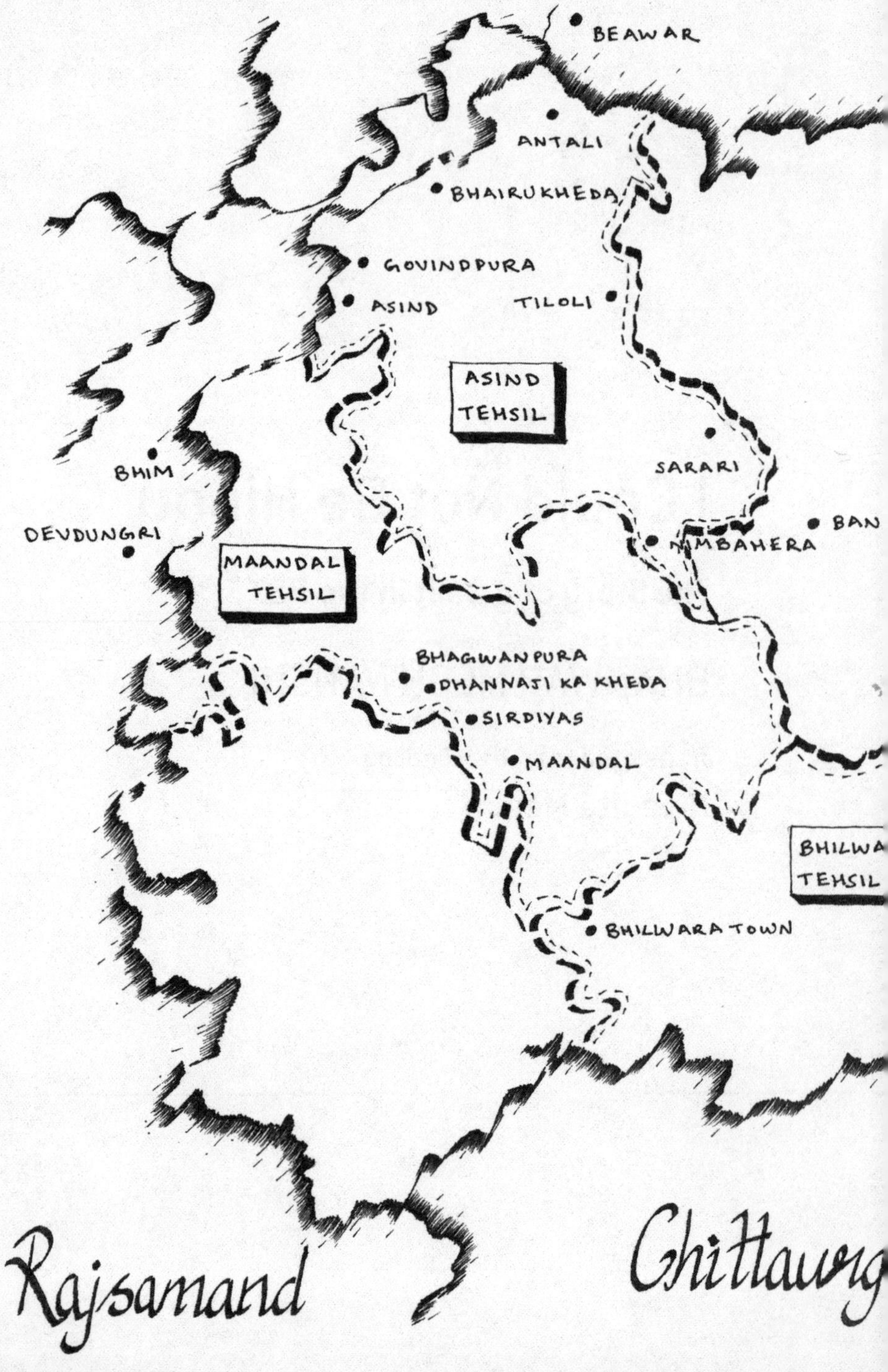

BEAWAR
ANTALI
BHAIRUKHEDA
GOVINDPURA
ASIND
TILOLI
ASIND TEHSIL
SARARI
BHIM
DEVDUNGRI
NIMBAHERA
BAN
MAANDAL TEHSIL
BHAGWANPURA
DHANNAJI KA KHEDA
SIRDIYAS
MAANDAL
BHILWA TEHSIL
BHILWARA TOWN
Rajsamand
Chittaurg

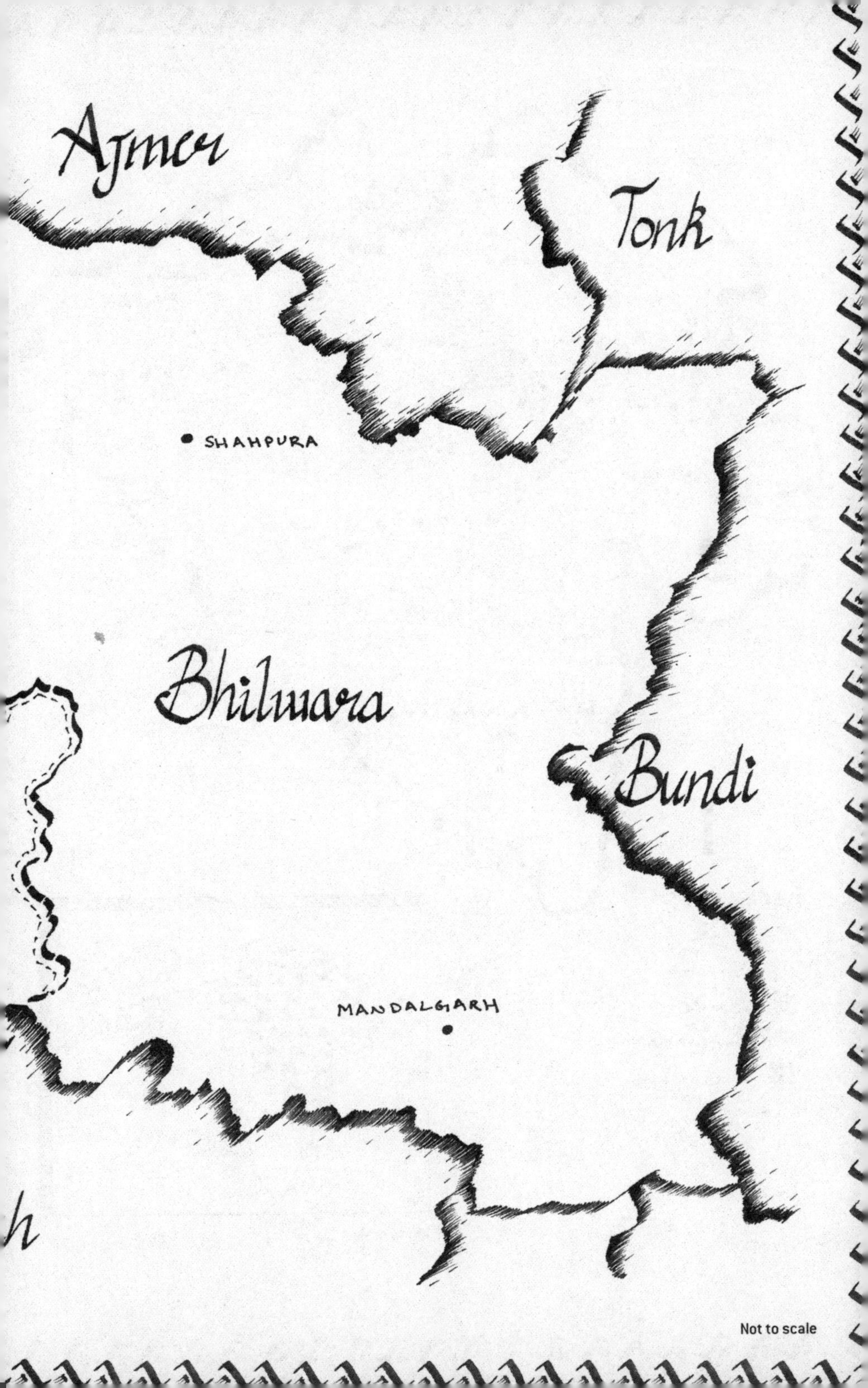

Ajmer

Tonk

SHAHPURA

Bhilwara

Bundi

MANDALGARH

h

Not to scale

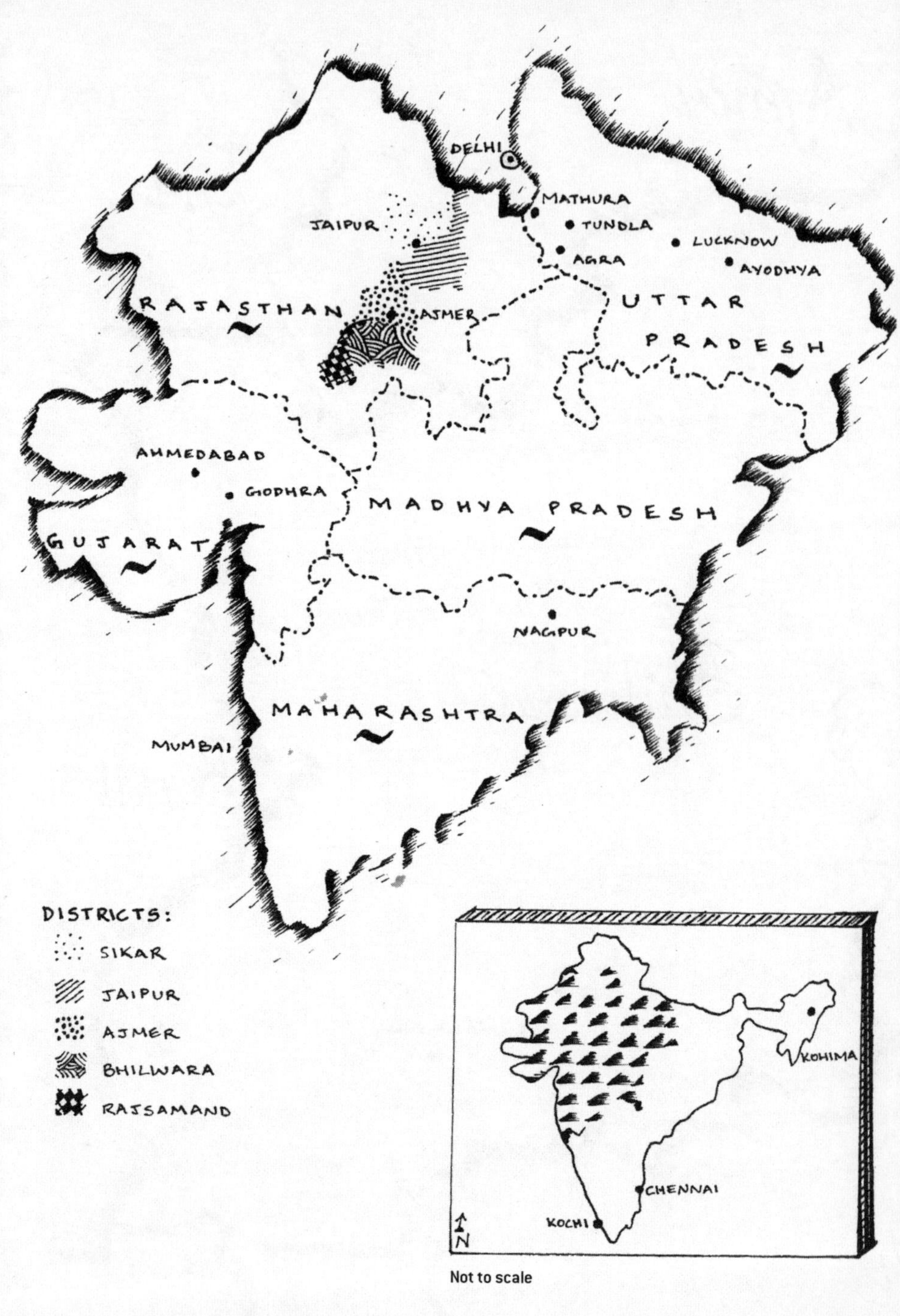
DELHI
MATHURA
TUNDLA
JAIPUR
LUCKNOW
AGRA
AYODHYA
RAJASTHAN
AJMER
UTTAR
PRADESH
AHMEDABAD
GODHRA
MADHYA PRADESH
GUJARAT
NAGPUR
MAHARASHTRA
MUMBAI
DISTRICTS:
SIKAR
JAIPUR
AJMER
BHILWARA
RAJSAMAND
KOHIMA
CHENNAI
KOCHI
N

Not to scale

Contents

1

We swear in the name of Ram!

I'm speaking of the days when the Ramjanmabhoomi–Babri Masjid dispute was at fever pitch, the air ringing with slogans like

> *Baccha baccha Ram ka/ janmabhoomi ke kaam ka.*
> Every child must prove his worth/ Work for the place of Ram's birth.
>
> *Janmabhoomi ke kaam na aaye, vo bekaar jawaani hai!*
> If it does not serve His place of birth, one's youth has no worth!
>
> *Jis Hindu ka khoon na khaule/ khoon nahin vo paani hai.*
> Hindu blood that does not seethe with anger/ is not blood, it's just water.

It was October 1990. I was about fifteen years old, studying in class ten. We were conducting a campaign for the Ram temple at Ayodhya in my village Sirdiyas in Maandal tehsil and in my home town Bhilwara. Bricks to build the temple had already been sanctified with prayer. I was desperate to join karseva, the actual work of building the temple at the birthplace of Ram, and to prove my credentials as a true swayamsevak, an activist of the Rashtriya Swayamsevak Sangh. The opportunity finally arrived when I was included in a contingent ready to give its life for the temple. Without letting my family know, I ran away to join the karseva. Before we set out for Ayodhya, we organised processions in different places in Maandal. I was exhilarated. I remember people wearing garlands, a saffron band tied around their heads, a blood red tika on the forehead, fists raised to chants of *Jai Shri Ram, Jai jai Shri Ram*, their voices rending the sky. On our lips were the words:

> *Ram-ji ke naam par jo mar jaayenge, duniya mein naam apna amar kar jaayenge.*
> To die for Ram-ji is such an honour, your name will ring in every corner.

I was certain we would be confronted by the anti-Hindu police of 'Mulla'-yam Singh, and that we would readily give our lives to liberate the birthplace of Maryada Purushottam Ram, the peerless among men. We set out for Ajmer by train in October 1990. There, in a choultry, we met up with thousands of others, all in saffron headbands. All of us hoped to reach the sacred birthplace and destroy that symbol of slavery, the Babri Masjid. Leaders of the RSS and the Vishwa Hindu Parishad were also present, and after our meal, they gathered us together and exhorted us to reach Ayodhya at all costs. In case the Mulayam Singh government took steps to suppress or stop us, whether by arrests or any other measures, they taught us how to evade the police, fool them and keep moving ahead. The senior leaders who spoke were clear in their instructions, that even at the cost of our lives, we must meet our objective of wiping out that stain of slavery, the Babri Masjid.

My heart longed to soar instantly to the Lord's city of Ayodhya and free the Infant Ram from the clutches of the outcaste infidels. How much longer were we to tolerate the presence of that structure of slavery in our own land, the land of Hindus, and at the very birthplace of our revered deity? We had already received directions to proceed on our mission whatever the cost. We were told that implements to destroy the structure—hoes, spades, crowbars—would be provided by the locals at Ayodhya.

In the evening, we caught the train to Lucknow. In the contingent from Bhilwara were many well-known faces of the RSS, VHP and the Bharatiya Janata Party, and their presence encouraged our fervour. I thanked Lord Ram in my heart for giving me this amazing opportunity, to be chosen with such famous people for His work. It felt as if every person there was eager to be martyred for Ram. All differences among people had been erased—young and old, rich and poor, ordinary and privileged, we had become as one. There were those who had given up everything— status, great wealth, factories, big houses, high posts—to do Lord Ram's work. Oh Ram-ji, the world is but your divine illusion!

It was like a second battle for independence. We were freedom fighters. How heroic we felt. In joyous agitation we boarded the train. Each had his ticket, so that if we got separated, we could still carry on. The station was packed with people, well-wishers here to see others off outnumbered the actual travellers. Raised fists, inflamed faces, roars of *Jai jai Shri Ram, vande mataram, jaykaare Bajrangi, har har Mahadev....* I had never before encountered such uproar, such excitement. The whistle blew. One more time we raised our fists and shouted *We swear upon Ram, we will build the temple there.* Our journey to Ayodhya had begun.

As the train started to slide out of the station, all the important functionaries slid out of the train. What was happening? Why were they getting off? Will the pracharaks of the RSS stay back too? Won't they go with us? I saw how one by one, the big folk, the industrialists, the sangh pracharaks, the leaders of the VHP and BJP, all excused themselves. Having wished us well, they went back to their homes. Only people like me remained—impassioned Dalits, Adivasis, other young people from the lower castes, and a few sadhus and sants, sages and ascetics. To take charge of us, some lower-order functionaries tried to put us at ease: Don't worry, these people have other contingents to see off and then they'll follow us directly to Ayodhya. They were never to come, they were sensible people and went back to their homes. I understood that sensible people always use us, we who are driven by passion; they push us into battle and return to their safe little coops. In this lies their greatness; maybe greatness is just another word for cunning.

2

Hatred towards travellers of other faiths

The exit of the big guns left us somewhat uncomfortable, a little sad, disappointed. But as the train picked up speed, our disappointment faded. At the next station, local people were waiting to welcome us; we were given fruit, tea, beedis, chewing tobacco. Everyone was elated. The train was mostly karsevaks, and the few regular passengers sat quiet, intimidated. There were also a few Muslims in our compartment. Seeing them, we started shouting: *If it's in India that you want to stay/ Vande Mataram is what you must say.* We glared at them menacingly. We wanted to throw them off the train, these infidels because of whom our Lord Ram was imprisoned in a derelict monument. *Our* land, *our* Ram, and these people prevent us from building a temple in His birthplace! We Hindus, second-class citizens in our own country; and these outcastes, living it up. Each one marries four women, and how they keep multiplying, breeding armies of their kind. Because of them Partition, but at least it rid us of half of them. This lot remains—left behind to sit astride our chests and torment us! Such thoughts stoked my hatred of the Muslim passengers, my rage was so great that if I had a weapon, even before liberating Ramjanmabhoomi, I would have taken care of these Yavana, Mughal, Pathan infidels, liberated them from their lives. At least some of the burden on Ma Bharati, Mother India, would be eased. The Muslim passengers must have been terrorised by our hate-filled stares, and seeing them like that—frightened, cowering—thrilled us. For once, we felt we had shown them their place.

It was a good thing they stayed silent, or who knows what may have happened. Slowly, the night deepened and sleep weighed down our eyelids. The commotion of slogans, bhajans and keertans, our collective hymn-singing, began to subside as the karsevaks fell asleep. Karsevak was the name given by our leaders to those who were going to perform their religious duty voluntarily, with their own hands. The duty of building the Ram temple at Ayodhya.

I was still half-awake, and saw that the other passengers were looking relieved, or less tense now, at this respite from the attention of Ram's devotees. Then I too fell asleep, a sweet deep sleep, in which I dreamt of entering Lord Ram's city Saket by the banks of the Sarayu, a dream that was on the verge of coming true.

3

First trip to jail

I slept soundly till dawn, when a commotion at a station called Tundla woke me up. There was great agitation among the karsevaks. The police had stopped the train. It looked like we wouldn't be allowed to go ahead. The police started an inspection. Each of us had to hand over our ticket and get off at the station, which had become a sea of roaring, maddened karsevaks, shouting: *The whole world may try and stop us/ But Infant Ram, we will reach you!*

Our oath was in vain. This Mulla-yam's government had indeed stopped us. We were all arrested. The night was fading, and in the light of the approaching day we found ourselves packed like sheep into police trucks. First we were taken to the Mathura Inter College, but that was already full, so we were moved to Agra's multipurpose stadium, where a provisional jail camp had been set up. But here, too, were more people than could be accommodated. About eighty of us were left out in the end. Before they could move us again, we began shouting to be placed here. We yelled our slogans and refused to be moved. Eventually we were packed anyhow into the temporary jail.

As we entered, we saw that the jail was a huge ground with tents, the walls so low that anybody could jump over them. But where could we have gone, with Agra under curfew, the police sure to come after us, the place unknown? All our great, respected big brothers (bhaisahabs) who had inspired us to martyr ourselves for the temple had left us at Ajmer and gone back. We here were the passionate youth, the sadhu–sants who had given up the world, the opium addicts, the marijuana smokers. Many of them had in fact already started smoking ganja and were soon lost in its fumes.

So, it was just us and the makeshift jail. The tent above our heads, durries under us, watery dal mixed with grit, burnt rotis, foul-tasting water, taunts and insults from the police. Somehow we got through our first ten days of jail life. We had set out for the birthplace of Ram, but ended up in the birthplace of Krishna—a prison! Still, we felt immense pride that we had been jailed for Shri Ram. We were karsevaks, the real goods.

4

Insults, stones, attacks, fear and stench

In the end, we were released after our names and addresses had been noted, and a stamp put on our hands. That jail was really no jail at all. Daily meetings of the Sangh, called shakhas, were held regularly, along with lots of discussion, hymns and religious discourses from the sadhu–sant crew. It didn't feel like a jail. When we were released, there were no trucks to transport us, we were just set loose. The town was still under curfew. We decided to walk along the railway tracks to the station, and headed towards Agra Cantonment. The would-be martyred were a bit tired. The karseva had not succeeded. We heard that Mulla-yam Singh had ordered police firing on karsevaks at the bridge over the Sarayu in Ayodhya. Many had died, many were injured, and others had thrown themselves into the swift-flowing Sarayu to escape bullets, but lost their lives in the process. Given the powerful police presence, not a soul could have passed undetected; our project of swarming over the Babri Masjid was a non-starter. Mulayam Singh indeed proved to be a 'Mulla'–'Yama' for the karsevaks.

Defeated, deeply disappointed and depressed, we were creeping along the tracks when suddenly in front of us appeared about a dozen people shouting *Jai Shri Ram*. We thrilled back to life again. Imagine, despite the curfew, devotees of Ram had come out to welcome us! A spring returned to our steps, our enthusiasm was renewed.

But what was this…? They were Muslims, with stones in their hands. And it was no more *Jai Shri Ram* on their lips, but abuse—*mother……, sister……, did you come here to grab your ….? Kill the mother……s!* We were stunned. Darkness was upon us. We looked around for help, but everywhere we saw hostility. The settlements along the tracks were Muslim areas. We got into a scuffle with the young men in front of us. Some of us were hurt, our bags fell to the ground, and they beat one of us mercilessly. He was heavy-built, couldn't run. The rest ran after us, throwing stones. We managed to stay just ahead, with them in hot pursuit.

We made it to the railway police station. The inspector in charge emerged, another Yadav, of the lineage of Mulla-yam, and from his divine lips too issued choice abuse. In front of us, holding lathis, stood the police to whom we had turned for help, and behind us were stone-throwing Muslims! Oh god, oh Ram, what do we do now? Save us! It felt as if death was inevitable. But where the Ram votive failed, we were saved by the locomotive. We slipped into the wagons of a stationary goods train, shut the doors and thus saved our lives. Finally the angry Muslim youth left, as did the police. Heaving sighs of relief, we got out on to the station, and a while later, caught a train headed for Jaipur. It was packed. We could only find space to stand near the toilet. And of course, we had no tickets.

Between the pressure of the crowd, our fear, and the hideous stench from the toilets—we felt overwhelmed. The desire to martyr ourselves for karseva was the real martyr of the day. We just wanted to get back home now. Meanwhile, our folks at home were in a bad way, having heard the news from Ayodhya. My brother Badrilal and I had both embarked upon karseva, and my parents were certain we had fallen to police bullets, leaving them childless. Well, neither did we die for Ram-ji, nor did they become childless. In fifteen days we were back home, alive and perfectly well.

5

In the RSS shakha

I didn't really learn any lesson from this experience, because while the intoxication of karseva may have worn off, the madness of nationalism was still upon me. It was a madness that gripped me as early as the age of thirteen, while I was still a student of class six. I had enrolled in the RSS then. It happened this way. The geography teacher of my government school in Nimbahera, Banshilal Sen, started organising sports for us in the village grounds. He sang very well too, and made us do physical exercises. We loved it all. First some games, then exercise. A couple of songs, followed by some edifying words. There were bits in the advice I did not fully understand, some of it even disturbed me. For instance, as a geography teacher in class, he taught us that the sun is a ball of fire, nobody can go close to it, they would burn up in its heat. But during sports, while teaching us the surya namaskar, the sun salutation, he made us chant prayers to the sun—*Om suryaya namah, ravaye namah, om savitr surya narayanaya namah*—telling us the story of how Hanuman had swallowed the sun whole. He would proudly say, see how powerful was our Bajrangbali Hanuman, who could swallow up the sun god and plunge the entire universe into darkness. This puzzled and disturbed me, and one day I plucked up the courage to ask, 'Gurudev, is the sun a god or a ball of fire?' His reply was, 'My boy, in the shakha the sun is a god, in school he is a ball of fire.' I was even more confused. I asked, 'But then how did Hanuman-ji swallow the sun?' He replied, 'Bajrangbali is extraordinarily powerful, the sun was just a ball of fire. Such was Bajrangbali's might that not only did he take the sun into his mouth, he was about to chew it up when, alarmed by the darkness that descended upon all the worlds, the other gods intervened and begged Hanuman to let the sun go. Only then did he relent.'

After this my belief in Hanuman-ji became unshakeable. I started finding geography ridiculous. During the geography class, I would mentally recite the "Hanuman Chalisa", a hymn of forty verses to Hanuman. I knew this subject was pointless, the reality was Hanuman's strength. In any case, Guru-ji had already told us in the shakha that those who doubt will perish: *sanshayaatma vinashyati*. I gave up all doubt, and entered an era of faith while still very young. Guru-ji also turned me away from science, and my belief in religious rites grew. Guru-ji taught us that our religion was the best, that these sessions of sports and exercise and teachings were part of a shakha of the Rashtriya Swayamsevak Sangh. He told us this was a new branch of the RSS that had opened in our village of Sirdiyas, and we young boys were its twigs. There were about fifty of us. We came from all castes, even those who considered people of my kind to be beneath them and wouldn't even talk to us properly. But here we all addressed one another as 'ji'. From plain Bhanwar I too became Bhanwar-ji, well on my way to becoming Bhanwar-ji bhaisahab.

Of the fifty or so children who attended the shakha in my village, most were OBCs—Kumhar, Jat, Gurjar, Mali and so on. From among Dalits, there were Bunkars and Dholis, and also a couple of Bhil Adivasis. The entire village was of course organised around caste. My school too. It was less evident in the shakha but I gradually noticed that the chief activists were all from the so-called upper castes, people like us made rank-and-file swayamsevaks.

I started to internalise the RSS ideology very quickly. I read its literature, especially the mouthpiece *Panchjanya*, and picked up the terminology and language quite easily. I attended RSS functions not only in my village but participated actively even at tehsil and district level events. Perhaps this is why I started rapidly moving up in the hierarchy. While the other children did not even reach the tehsil (or taluka) level, I became quite popular with the RSS people and engaged the leaders in discussions. I realise now that they recognised my potential to become an ideologically sound RSS activist, and were systematically preparing me for it.

My progress was unexpectedly rapid. From gananayak (a ground-level 'leader of the people') I became the chief teacher, and soon reached the district headquarters where I was given the responsibility of being district office chief of the RSS.

6

An RSS shakha

A shakha, which in Hindi means 'branch', is the daily gathering of RSS swayamsevaks held for an hour or so in some clean public space. This takes place in the early morning, evening or at night, depending on the convenience of the swayamsevaks. For instance, traders would prefer an early morning shakha, students an evening one, for others, it could be at night, or even weekly shakhas instead of daily ones. For that matter, there are now WhatsApp shakhas—the point is that people should be active in the work of the Sangh and take out time for it. Of course, morning or evening shakhas are considered ideal and these are very popular. Recently we've been hearing of shakhas in IIMs even.

The hour is divided in the following way.

Opening and run – 5 minutes
Physical exercises – 10 minutes
Games – 20 minutes
Yoga – 10 minutes
Intellectual input – 10 minutes
Prayer – 5 minutes

The shakha begins with a whistle blown by the instructor, the shakha pramukh, at which the participants stop talking and, turning towards the saffron RSS flag, stand in the 'at ease' position.

After this, the pramukh calls out 'All alert!' (sangh daksh) and then 'At Ease!' (aaram). He next approaches each line, one by one. Standing before the leader of each, he shouts out the commands to maintain two steps distance from the next person by following the lead of the person in front of you (agresar samyak), then to stand at ease (aaram), and be ready to spring to attention when the order is given.

The order of agresar ardhvrit comes next, at which the leader turns around 180 degress towards the back, followed by everyone else; then the order to stand at ease, and then once again at attention. The saffron flag is hoisted and the order 'dhwaj pranam ek-do-teen' given which prompts our salute: Hands are placed on hearts, heads bowed. After this, the participants are counted, with the last person in each row going up to the leader of his line with the number.

The number is passed on to the pramukh while the participants stand at ease. This is the way daily attendance at the shakha is monitored. The command of attention follows, and then everyone takes their place at the order of svasthan.

The remaining activities of the day take place one by one, and finally the pracharak's whistle blows again, for the dispersal of the shakha. The prayer to the motherland is recited—*Namaste sada vatsale matrubhoomi*, there's another salute to the flag, which is then lowered, and finally, the order of dispersal is given. At this order, sangh vikir, the swayamsewaks turn to their right, bow and then disperse.

Every day the surya namaskar must be performed, beginning with the chant of *mitraya namah* and ending with *shri savitr surya narayanaya namah*. Other yogasanas we performed were tadasana (mountain pose), vrikshasana (tree), trikonasana (triangle), veerbhadrasana (warrior), vajrasana (thunderbolt), ushtrasana (camel), and shavasana (corpse pose).

The order to sit is upvish and the order to stand utthishth. Organising daily games is mandatory. There were several—Frog, Salutations, Tiger!, Namaskar, Kabaddi, The Demon of the Ashes, Bear Fight, The Dance of Death, Ram–Ravan, Crossing the River, Protecting a Friend, Fire Pit, The Leaping War God, Delhi is Ours….

Some games were played seated, such as—We shall Eat, Recognise the Leader, Post Office, Ramkrishna.

The Sangh celebrated six main festivals—among these Diwali, Holi, Republic Day and Independence Day were *not* included. What we did celebrate was Varsha Pratipad (Hindu New Year, and the RSS founder Hedgewar's birth anniversary, 1 April), Vijayadashami, Makar Sankranti (the day after the winter solstice that marks the harvest season in the subcontinent), Hindu Empire Day (the coronation day of Chattrapati Shivaji Bhonsle in 1774 as emperor, anointed by a Brahmin), Rakshabandhan (when among the Hindus of North India, sisters tie a protective amulet on the wrists of brothers) and Guru Poornima (at which a gift was always given to the teacher, and in this case donations were collected under the

RSS saffron flag in the name of the guru).

To participate in the shakha it was compulsory to wear a white shirt, black cap, belt, brown shoes and khaki shorts, this was our uniform. Each member of the shakha, or swayamsevak, had to buy the uniform, which was called ganvesh, the dress of the people, with his own money.

During the intellectual segment of the shakha, we had a short address in Sanskrit called subhashit; readings from the work of great people, called Amrit Vachan (Immortal Utterances); and sometimes a short lecture. We were taught to recite the *ekatmata stotra* and *ekatmata mantra* about the unity of Bharatvarsh. We sang songs like

> May the conch announcing Hindu Rashtra blow
> May the challenge rise from every pore
> May darkness be dispelled by the blaze of valour
> May Hindu and Hindusthan ascend forever.

We also learnt to shout slogans hailing Shivaji, Rana Pratap, the god Shiva as Mahadev, and the RSS leaders Madhav (Sadashiv Golwalkar) and Keshav (Baliram Hedgewar).

From the time I was in the village, to the time I reached Bhilwara, attending the shakha was an integral part of my day. My favourite shakhas were in Azad Nagar, Mukherjee Udyan and the garden of Mahatma Gandhi Hospital. We used to turn up at the morning shakhas, in full uniform, with our bamboo sticks, feeling like soldiers. The smallest unit of the shakha is the individual swayamsevak, above him the gatanayak, the group leader, then the chief teacher, who was at the head and gave all the orders. The structure and conduct of the shakha was very martial, and to tell the truth, I loved it. Also the way each of us had to call one another 'ji', old or young we had to show respect to each other, it felt spiritual and uplifting.

Even today, many of the shlokas we used to recite, and the songs we used to sing, remain in my memory, the way we used to recite the prayer before the saffron flag, standing at attention with our hands on our hearts—*Namaste sada vatsale matrubhoomi...* 'We bow to thee O ever-loving mother'.

There was a lot of emphasis on nationalism in the shakha, and anyway, my heart was filled with love for my country. I so loved the songs sung in the shakha that I knew them by heart:

> Stride forth, build the organisation
> Stride forth upon that noble track
> Of the work that builds the nation
> Let there never be a lack.

There were hymns to Bharat Mata:

> May your glory shine forever, Mother, long outlive our petty lives.

Then there was the shloka which I felt blessed to recite:

> Mother and motherland are greater than heaven itself.

And a poem by Ramavtar Tyagi:

This body is yours, this mind is yours, yours every pore
And still I wish, oh motherland, I could give you more.

These songs and poems were gloriously inspiring. Every day was like Holi or Diwali.

It seemed obvious to me that we who attended the shakha were the true patriots, the rest were clearly traitors.

7

Offering to the teacher, sharing meals

The expenses of the various functionaries and pracharaks of the Sangh, for accommodation, food, travel and so on are met by the offerings made to the flag on Guru Poornima, dedicated to honouring the guru or teacher. The amounts collected from the various shakhas reach the district headquearters, where the total collection is kept secure by some wealthy individual swayamsevak, from whom various sums are drawn from time to time.

A pracharak is a full-time Sangh activist who remains celibate, and a vistarak a part-time activist who enters family life (grihasthashram) and works in society to expand the network of the Sangh.

In Bhilwara, the Sangh's money was placed with a trader who lived on Sabun Road. The money was not used for personal expenses. The pracharak received no salary, his personal expenses were minimal. The money was used only for social welfare. The pracharak was expected to live an extremely simple life. With one set of clothes on his body and the RSS ganvesh or uniform in a bag, he was expected by the Sangh leadership to be totally focused on his official duties.

Most pracharaks did in fact lead such lives. There were also those who had become corrupt, who accepted personal wealth, who carried out business or political activities in their capacity as pracharak, but these people were not respected and were whispered about behind their backs.

In my time the district pracharak was an extremely principled man, Shiv-ji bhaisahab, who maintained strict discipline and lived a life of simplicity and frugality. He possessed only two sets of kurta–pyjama, and a small cloth bag. He slept on the ground, ate modestly, and was extremely punctual. He had no personal life, and spent most of his time touring the region. Always dressed in white, he lived austerely. Unlike the pracharaks of today, he did not get involved in politics, business and other such crooked schemes. Most pracharaks of the town were like Shiv-ji bhaisahab. Of course, at the time I had boundless respect for RSS pracharaks. I revered the bhaisahabs—these elder-brotherly mentor figures—and was not likely to notice anything wrong in whatever they did. Indeed, I remember now that there was a tehsil pracharak, Bhagwan-ji bhaisahab, who was involved in activities apart from the Sangh's work, and he went on to become a big businessman and political leader.

The district pracharak had a motorcycle on which he travelled across the district, and the money for petrol and daily expenses had to be picked up from Shyam-ji Daad, businessman and BJP leader, the one with the shop on Sabun Road. The district pracharak would write an amount on a piece of paper and sign it, and money would be given against his note. I was sent on this mission from time to time, but I never liked it. These traders and businessmen have a very high opinion of themselves; very well behaved towards those in a position to help them, and to those who need them, very harsh. At best, distant and formal, but too often uncouth. On receiving the pracharak's letter, they always released the money, but as if they were handing out alms. I hated the way they behaved as if they were doing us a big favour, when the money had come from swayamsevaks' contributions and they were merely its custodians.

Once I asked the pracharak why the amount collected from guru dakshina was not simply deposited in a bank, why depend on these Baniyas, who seem reluctant to part with any of it. In response he said, 'Friend, the money is safe with wealthy swayamsevaks, others might end up spending it out of need. This community has proved to be best at maintaining and accounting for money and that's why all over the country the guru dakshina collection is placed in their safekeeping. Nor has there been any complaint so far.'

I was convinced by his response and never again doubted the wisdom of this practice. I understood that this community was best equipped to manage the funds of the swayamsevaks. Every caste has been allotted a particular kind of work, and they are good at it, perhaps this is why our ancestors allotted occupations by caste.

So this is how expenses were dealt with by the Sangh, but food involved no expenses. All functionaries of the Sangh were expected to eat at different people's homes. Those of us who lived in the Sangh office prepared our own food, but sometimes we went with the pracharak when he was invited to a meal. Big businessmen and professionals considered it an honour to have the pracharak, whom we all called pujya bhaisahab (revered elder brother), over for a meal. The food was simple and tasty, and vegetarian.

We heard that pracharaks who were Kshatriya were permitted to eat meat, but never in the Sangh office or in public spaces such as the homes of Sangh supporters. At a personal level, everyone from the individual swayamsevak to the most honoured chief pracharak, or sarsanghchalak, was permitted to eat meat. In fact, certain enthusiasts believed that Hindus had become weak and cowardly because of their vegetarianism, and that meat was a must to build up physical strength and defeat the cruel enemy. But in the teachings of the Sangh and its activities this opinion did not hold sway, because the strongest supporters of the Sangh were Brahmins and Baniyas, who are vegetarian. Although there were some even among these who secretly enjoyed non-vegetarian food, in public they were vociferous in their support of vegetarianism, silencing opponents. I was born and raised a vegetarian and a vocal critic of meat-eating. My father never touched alcohol or meat, and never allowed these things into our home. So my birth made me a votary of vegetarianism, and this view was strengthened on my becoming the pujari of a temple; it was only much later that my opinion on this matter changed.

Since I lived in the Sangh office, I often visited homes of our supporters with the pracharak to share meals . But I was hesitant as well, because I always feared that someone would ask my caste and then his behaviour towards me would change. The fear was not without foundation, because this had indeed happened at a couple of homes, but I was expected to accompany the pracharak, and so I did. In addition I felt that urban hospitality lacked the spirit and warmth of villages; the interactions were formal and superficial, and the lack of spices and seasoning in the food also bored me. Sensing my state of mind, pracharak-ji one day explained to me why we went from home to home to share meals with different people.

He said that this practice of eating at homes was very special, it took the reach of the Sangh deep into society, and encouraged the family of the swayamsevak to get involved in the Sangh's work. Positive feelings towards the Sangh were generated by these encounters. The shakha linked individual swayamsevaks, while the home visits drew in families. This explanation, however, did not remove my hesitation and doubts about the practice.

Pracharak-ji once said to me that the Sangh functioned not in a proselytising or agitative manner, but rather its attempt was to reach out to individuals through friendship and warmth. To touch people individual by individual, to bring them to the shakha, go to their homes, eat with them, prepare them for our ideology—this is the style of the Sangh. This is why the Sangh calls itself a factory for the construction of individuals. By eating at homes, we meet and talk to every member of the family, and build a spiritual bond with them that is lifelong.

In this way the Sangh entered each family, brought our teaching to the hearts and minds of each person, and despite all setbacks and adverse circumstances, our work went on quietly. No outward drama, nothing visible to the world at large; just the quiet everyday infiltration of homes and minds, the collection of funds through guru dakshina. It was a difficult path to follow, requiring much patience with few immediate results, but this was our way. This was what we taught every day in the shakha.

8

Organisation of the Sangh

The Sangh has organised the country into eleven regions (kshetras) and forty-one districts (zilas) for its work. The regions are South, South–Central, West, Central, North–West, North, West–North–Central, East–North–Central, North–East, East and Assam.

The forty-one states are—Kerala, South and North Tamil Nadu, South and North Karnataka, West and East Andhra, Konkan, Western Maharashtra, Devgiri, Vidarbha, Gujarat, Malwa, Central India, Mahakaushal, Chhattisgarh, Chittor, Jaipur, Jodhpur, Delhi, Haryana, Punjab, Jammu–Kashmir, Himachal, Uttarakhand, Meerut, Braj, Kanpur, Avadh, Kashi, Gorakhpur, North and South Bihar, Jharkhand, Utkal, South and North Bengal, South and North Assam, Arunachal and Manipur.

Each administrative district has been further divided into two or three Sangh districts, and Sangh activists at various levels are appointed to each of these units. In addition, the different regions, that are now called 'Sangh Thought Family', have official post holders at every level. They are coordinated by pracharaks and headed by a liaison official, and all of them come together for regular monthly meetings at the Sangh office. The Sangh office in every district has a pracharak and a vistarak, and a store with the ganvesh, lathis, books and other material that can be purchased.

In this way, the Sangh has a smooth-functioning organisational machinery with three tiers. At the grassroot level, the individual swayamsevak is the fundamental unit of the Sangh upon whom the organisation rests, many of whom come together to form daily shakhas.

Above the swayamsevak, the gatanayak, gananayak, chief teacher, shakha manager (karyavah), and mandal official.

At the top, the organisation is like the confluence of the three holy rivers—pracharaks, karyavahs, and sanghchalaks in descending order. Thus city pracharak, city karyavah, city sanghchalak; zila pracharak, zila karyavah, zila sanghchalak and so on up to the level of the region. Then, in ascending order, the sarkaryavah (chief manager) and sarsanghchalak at the very top. The structures which obtain at the city and district level extend upwards through the departmental (vibhaagiya), provincial (praantiya) and regional (kshetriya) levels. The sarsanghchalak, or helmsman of the Sangh, is the supremo, and he is selected from among pracharaks alone. The other two categories, of the karyavah and sanghchalak, are not considered for this post. So far six pracharaks have become sarsanghchalak, of whom five are Brahmin (Keshav Baliram Hedgewar, 'Guru-ji' M.S. Golwalkar, Madhukar Dattatraya 'Balasaheb' Deoras, K.S. Sudarshan, Mohan Bhagwat) and one Kshatriya (Rajendra Singh, known as Rajju Bhaiyya). In the Sangh, posts are filled by nomination, not election, as the Sangh is thought to work like a family, where the choice made in consultation among elders is more acceptable than elections. The post of sarsanghchalak used to be for life, but this has changed.

Questions have been raised—never from within the Sangh, only from outside—about the fact that the sarsanghchalak has mostly been Brahmin. Only those who have no clue about the organisation and functioning of the RSS could even raise this question. Only a pracharak who has reached the top of the hierarchy would be considered for sarsanghchalak, and at the top Dalits, Adivasis and Backward Castes are negligible in number. Under the circumstances, there is no chance of any of them becoming sarsanghchalak for the next fifty years.

Forget about becoming sarsanghchalak, there is very little participation by Dalits and Adivasis even in the top national level organisational units such as the All India Representatives Assembly (Akhil Bharatiya Pratinidhi Sabha) or the All India Working Committee (Akhil Bharatiya Karyakari Mandal). Over the last two decades, ever since this question has arisen, the RSS has been very aware that marginalised communities should be given organisational responsibilities in the different outfits of the Sangh parivar or family. However, the actual presence of such groups at the national levels of the organisation is still barely noticeable.

Dalits and backward groups had participated enthusiastically in the 1990 and 1992 karseva campaigns, and the Sangh leadership too had paid special attention to young men of these groups. There had been special attempts to bring them into shakhas and to give them responsibilities in various fronts of the Sangh, but despite such conscious efforts, very few Dalits have become pracharaks, and they remain at the low to middling levels of the district and department. That no Dalit or Adivasi heads even one of the subsidiary organisations of the Sangh is a matter of grave concern for the leadership.

If one studies the All India Working Committee even after 2000, most post-holders are Brahmin, some Bania or Kshatriya and a couple of people from Backward Castes; there's not a single Dalit or Adivasi. The reason for this is clear—no Dalit or Adivasi has managed to reach the national level of the organisation. How then will Dalits and Adivasis be part of a Hindu Rashtra? This is the challenging question.

The example of Ramnath Kovind, president of India, is revealing. He belongs to an 'untouchable' caste, rose high in the BJP, and has now reached the highest constitutional post in the country, but never made the cut to be considered for the highest post in the unconstitutional RSS.

9

The Sangh is everywhere

The daily shakha is meant to build the individual, but the Sangh's larger agenda is to reach every limb of the social body and to control it. To this end, there are multiple organisations it has established. First, a women's organisation was founded in 1936 and Lakshmibai Kelkar appointed as its leader. She was universally known as mausi-ji, Aunty. She then set up the Rashtriya Sevika Samiti, for women, since they could not be part of the mainline RSS. When I first heard of this organisation, I wondered why the word swayam (self) was missing from its name, thus making its members 'servants' of others rather than of the self. Swayamsevak denotes volunteering, an autonomous volition, while sevika evokes a menial position of waiting on others. I asked several senior people but received no satisfactory reply, until I realised on my own that men can decide what to do with their 'self' but women must serve others. In any case the seniors of the Sangh believed that Doctor Sahab (Hedgewar, the founder) did right by not permitting women into the Sangh, that it was a good strategic move, because women in the Sangh would have by now ensured its destruction.

Not only was there a separate organisation for women, but for workers, Dalits, Adivasis, farmers, writers, intellectuals, journalists, film-makers. The idea was that the basic philosophy and form of the Sangh should not be diluted by these energies, they should be kept separate so that the Sangh's factory for shaping individuals could carry on its production unimpeded.

In 1948, the students' organisation Akhil Bharatiya Vidyarthi Parishad was formed at every level from schools to colleges and universities, in order to bring students together and intervene in student politics. In time this organisation became the stormtroopers of a political party, but its primary responsibility is to the Sangh.

In 1952, the Vanvasi Kalyan Ashram (Forest-dwellers' Welfare Body) was founded by Balasahab Deshpande, purportedly for the uplift of marginalised forest dwellers, but primarily in order to challenge the Christian missionaries who were working to convert innocent Adivasis. The forest dwellers were given the name of girijan or forest folk, but in time the use of terms like harijan and girijan became contested so the Sangh stopped using the term.

After Gandhi's assassination and the role in it imputed to the Sangh, many kinds of legal hurdles were placed in its functioning. Socially too, the Sangh felt the need for political support as it had become 'untouchable' for all political parties. It was under these circumstances that the second sarsanghchalak, Guru-ji Golwalkar, began to envisage a political party affiliated directly to the Sangh. Around this time, Syama Prasad Mookerjee resigned from the Nehru cabinet and directly asked for the Sangh's help in setting up a political party. This proposal was enthusiastically received by Guru-ji and others in the Sangh who believed that the time had come for a political intervention. Pandit Deendayal Upadhyay and Syama Prasad Mookerjee were deputed to this task. In 1951, a political party called the Bharatiya Jana Sangh came into formal existence. The founding president was Mookerjee and Deendayal Upadhyay the general secretary. After 1953, when Mookerjee passed away, the party came under the direct control of the Sangh. In 1967, the Jana Sangh participated in coalition governments with other parties in several states. In 1975, in opposition to the Emergency, the it joined the JP movement (a movement for 'total revolution' launched by the socialist leader Jayaprakash Narayan), and eventually merged with the Janata Party, becoming part of a short-lived government. In 1980, the Bharatiya Janata Party was formed under the leadership of Atal Bihari Vajpayee and Lal Krishna Advani. From two seats in the Lok Sabha at that time, the BJP is in full majority today with swayamsevak Narendrabhai Damodardas Modi as prime minister. This is the fruit of the Sangh's long-term strategy, although the RSS claims again and again to be only a social and cultural organisation and not a political one. From the Jana Sangh to the BJP, the RSS has concentrated its energies on nurturing a political party born of its beliefs, and the political control the Sangh now has at the Centre is a direct result of these efforts.

After its intervention in electoral politics, a trade union, the Bharatiya Mazdoor Sangh, was set up in 1955 under the senior pracharak and economist Dattopant Thengadi, in order to counter the Left's influence on workers. A large part of Sangh supporters were traders and businessmen, and they felt it necessary to bind the workers in their businesses to their own interests. The slogan of the BMS was: *We labour for the nation/ and demand full remuneration.* A similar organisation was started for farmers, the Bharatiya Kisan Sangh.

Meanwhile, Saraswati Shishu Mandirs had been established to educate children in Sangh ideology. In 1977, the Gorakhpur Saraswati Shishu Mandir transformed into Vidya Bharati, and the Vidya Bharati network of schools spread rapidly all over the country. It is difficult to find a taluka today without a Sangh-run school. There are 13,067 schools, 1,50,190 teachers and 34,75,757 students in its network, according to the Vidya Bharati website. Second only to the daily shakhas, the Adarsh Vidya Mandirs and Saraswati Shishu Mandirs are among the greatest strengths of the Sangh family.

For wealthy supporters who cannot come to the shakhas but want to contribute to the Sangh financially, the Bharat Vikas Parishad was founded in 1963, and for the more religiously inclined, the Vishwa Hindu Parishad in 1964.

The programme of setting up new organisations carries on till today. There are about a hundred such organisations: devoted to cultural and general research, some to the rewriting of history and science, to Sanskrit, one to foster social harmony (Samrasata Manch) where Dalits find a place, for Sikh welfare, for religious awakening, for indigenous economics, platforms for lawyers, traders, doctors and ex-servicemen, for small businesses, several medical and health missions, a handful of outfits dedicated to cow protection, as well as the better-known Bajrang Dal for young men to rouse rabble and the Durga Vahini for women.

In order to reach larger numbers of people, the Sangh has also set up several publishing houses. These include Bharat Prakashan, Suruchi Prakashan, Lokhit Prakashan, Gyan Ganga Prakashan, Archana Prakashan, Bharatiya Vichar Sadhana, Kalpataru, Shri Bharati Prakashan, Apna Sahitya, Sadhna Pustak Prakashan, Sahitya Niketan, Jagaran Prakashan, Rashtrotthan Sahitya; and publications like *Hindustan Samachar, Swadesh, Motherland, Organiser, Panchjanya* and *Rashtra Dharma*.

In addition to this, at local levels, the Sangh runs social organisations under different names. It is now an indisputable fact that without being formally registered, the Sangh is the world's largest NGO. Organisations run on Sangh ideology receive the lion's share of their funding from all over the world. Although the Sangh does not accept the identity of an NGO, nor does it take funding directly, organisations linked to the Sangh have been fundraising on a massive scale, but they never come under question. The nationalism label is a powerful charm.

10

I wanted to become a black cat

The RSS believes that it shapes the character of people in its shakhas. A person trained by them is like a black cat, which, however it is flung about and wherever life throws it, will always land on its feet. I wanted to be the black cat of the RSS. I put all my heart into the activities of the shakha.

It was in the shakha that I first beheld the portrait of Bharat Mata, Mother India, with the saffron flag in her hand. I wondered how it was that Bharat Mata held not the national tricolour but the Sangh's saffron flag. I received the answer, 'The tricolour was accepted as the national flag only after independence in 1947, but the saffron flag is from ancient times. That's why the lotus hands of Ma Bharati are resplendent with our proud saffron.'

Discipline was taken very seriously in the shakha. It was said that only by being strictly disciplined like soldiers could we build the nation. Our aim was the militarisation of Hinduism and the Hinduisation of the military. Thus, every instruction given in the shakha, termed 'commandment', was given in military style. But the orders were in Sanskrit, rather than the recognisable commands used all over the country.

For example, it was daksh (alert) for saavdhan (attention) and aaram for vishram (at ease). In school my Sanskrit teacher had impressed upon us that Sanskrit was no ordinary language, it was the language of the gods. All the divine Indian texts were composed in Sanskrit—*Vedas, Upanishads, Ramayana, Mahabharata*. This understanding had such an influence on me that when I heard orders given in Sanskrit, they seemed to me like orders directly from the gods.

Along with games and sports in the shakha, there was an intellectual component. When the physical activity had exhausted us, we would sit in a half circle and there would be a discussion. This was termed bauddhik, intellection. The discussion was conducted in a highbrow Sanskritised Hindi that spoke to my head and heart. It took the form of questions and answers, in which questions were asked like 'Who are we, whose is this country, who considers this their motherland?' Then the answers would be given, 'We, of pure Aryan blood, are Hindus, of Sanatana dharma, the eternal, most ancient religion, this country is ours, only we Hindus consider this our motherland, the land in which we are fulfilled through work. This country is our sacred pilgrimage. Since ancient times our land was a bird of gold. Rivers of milk ran here, and of curd and ghee. We were the gurus of the universe. We were invaded by the Shakas, Huns, Kushanas, Yavanas, Mughals, Pathans and Britishers. They looted our wealth and made us slaves. Other than Hindus, no community considers Bharat as their mother, or as their sacred pilgrimage. For some their sacred place is Jerusalem, for others it is Mecca–Medina. Only for us Hindus is everything here in Bharat. Only we are the true sons of Mother India.'

Hearing this, I would feel anger towards other communities, these people who ate the fruit of our land, but sang of Jerusalem and Mecca–Medina. I began to have serious doubts about their devotion to our nation.

Our shakha met between six and seven in the evening every day. At first only the geography teacher used to be there, but gradually other teachers started coming too. Sometimes big leaders would join us from the district and regional headquarters, we called them bhaisahab. My understanding was also enhanced by the literature available at the shakha. I gradually became more and more of a nationalist. I was filled with pride about being Hindu and of pure Aryan blood, and I began to look down on people following other faiths.

11

Khaki shorts, military shoes, some shlokas

It was compulsory for the chief teacher of the shakha to come in ganvesh, the full Sangh uniform. I too asked for money from my family and got myself the complete outfit—loose khaki shorts, black cap, leather belt, brown socks, black shoes and a bamboo staff, called dand, that came up to my ears. I already had a white shirt, so didn't need to buy that. Now that I was the chief teacher, I wore the ganvesh to the shakha every day. My family had never been of the ideology of the RSS or its electoral offshoot, the Jana Sangh. In fact, my grandfather and father had been opponents of this ideology. I was the stark contradiction of this. They had not really questioned me when I began to go to play in the shakha, but now that I was going daily in full Sangh uniform, my father started to challenge me. He told me these people have never been true to us, and nor will they ever be, I should stop going there. But I was so intoxicated by nationalism that even a mild questioning of the Sangh made me doubt a person's loyalty to the nation. My older brother and cousins mocked me mercilessly about the loose khaki shorts, but I put up with it.

My big brother Badri-ji has a very different relationship

with Hindutva politics. We are two brothers, with no sisters, and Badri-ji is the older by three years. As a six-month-old, he was adopted by my father's older brother Gokul-ji, and he grew up within that family. He never had any direct connection with the RSS, and joined karseva at my urging, motivated also by our agricultural supervisor, Rameshwar Lal Totla. Later he joined the BJP, but could never get on with the RSS, so he never rose in the party, remaining at the level of the Tehsil Working Committee. Eventually he became a contractor and went into the transport business, and is now the Bhilwara District Chairperson of the Dalit Indian Chambers of Commerce and Industry.

Those days I made every effort to learn Sanskrit. I knew many shlokas by heart, which I could recite flawlessly in one continuous stream. I began to consult the panchang, the Hindu calendar of special dates and festivals, while the *Bhagawad Gita*, the "Sundar Kand" of Tulsidas' *Ramcharit Manas* and the "Hanuman Chalisa" had all become a part of my daily schedule. In the shakha we used to recite the prayer 'We bow to thee O ever-loving mother'. We had not yet been assigned a saffron flag at our shakha, so we used to recite the prayer in a circle around a dot on the ground, imagining a saffron flag fluttering there. Under its imagined shade we sang praises of Bharat Mata. We were told that human minds were unpredictable in their emotions, but the saffron flag was the symbol of steadiness, purity and asceticism, and it should never be dishonoured in any way. This is why the Sangh considered the flag our guru. We were taught that this flag, bearing the colour of the holy flame, was the very image of sacrifice. The Sangh believed it was not individuals who had priority, but principles, so the place of the guru was occupied, not by any individual, but by the symbol of purity and principles, the saffron flag itself.

It had been six months since the shakha had been set up in the village. When the festival of Vijayadashami arrived, the district pracharak announced that our shakha would be granted the saffron flag. We were ecstatic. We would no longer be nigura, an abandoned guru-less mob.

Soon enough a tall iron rod, a stand and a flag in saffron cotton were presented to us. We made our first payment of guru dakshina, or gift to the guru, that day. The Sangh is an independent nationalist organisation, and its expenses are met by annual collections made from its volunteers on Guru Poornima, when everybody places an amount in an envelope and presents it to the flag. This is called guru dakshina. Our pracharak told us that the Sangh does not accept money from any other source.

My questioning mind would not be silent even on this occasion, and I couldn't help asking how a lifeless object like the flag could guide us the way a guru should. Banshilal Sen, my geography teacher, who was also the tehsil service chief, laughingly replied with the story of a Vedic sage who accepted as his guru twenty-four objects and animals—plants, trees, rivers, dogs, cats. So sublime is our Hindu culture, so generous, so expansive. Why then should we not accept the saffron flag as our guru? My doubts were stilled. Sangh activists always had instances from ancient times and ready answers to all questions. From that day forward, I accepted the saffron flag as my guru and the bamboo staff as my companion. The rest of my journey as a swayamsevak carried on in this way, with all my questions receiving answers, my arguments facing counter-arguments. The RSS prizes faith over doubt. This I had come to understand.

In informal conversations and gossip, an occasional reference to differences of opinion among the leaders did crop up, but the discipline of the organisation was so strong we never learned what the differences were about, and they were certainly never aired in public.

Once I turned to ask a pracharak: After all, Hindus are the majority in India, how can we be insecure? My confusion arose because in my village there was not a single Muslim or a person of any religion other than Hinduism. We had never heard the call of azan, or seen namaz being offered. It was difficult for me to imagine people of this community as my enemy. I asked my question, and pat came the answer, 'Even the Father of the Nation Mahatma Gandhi had said that Hindus are peace-loving cowards, and Muslims aggressive goons. One can never trust them not to betray us, and that's why despite being in the majority, we Hindus are not safe even in our own country.' I was convinced by this answer and understood that people of other faiths are the enemies of Hindus.

Other swayamsevaks may have had such doubts, but if so, did not raise them publicly. Many also came from families where Islamophobia was commonplace, but this was not so in my family and I found these views hard to swallow initially.

12

Panchjanya made a fanatic of me

Some literature came free to the shakha. The Sangh publication *Pathey Kan*, published fortnightly from Jaipur, cost thirty rupees annually. Other small booklets published by the RSS also arrived off and on, and were sold for prices between two and five rupees. I read Sita Ram Goel's pamphlet, *Hindu Samaj Khatre Mein* (Hindu Society in Danger), which disturbed me greatly. It revealed in detail the conspiracy that Muslims, Christians and communists were plotting against Hindus. The poor Hindu community was encircled by these forces.

My hunger for knowledge was growing. I became a regular subscriber to the weekly *Panchjanya* and read it eagerly, poring over every issue as if it was a religious text. If an issue did not arrive, the week seemed empty and meaningless. The fact is, my recognition and understanding of the Sangh's Hindu Nation grew out of the pages of the *Panchjanya*. Today I can admit that it was the *Panchjanya* that made me an ideological and intellectual fanatic in the cause of this Hindu Rashtra. Of course, my fanaticism was also fostered by the regular activities of the Sangh, as well as by participating in its training camps of five days (Initial Training Camps or ITCs) and twenty days (Officer Training Camps or OTCs). The discipline in these camps was intense. Exhausting physical exercise and training in wielding knives, lathis, swords, supposedly for self-defence. For the duration of the camp, participants were not permitted to leave the premises and meet anyone outside. There was an air of secrecy, to keep our activities away from the eyes of the media. It was said that the quality of a true swayamsevak was selfless service to the nation, away from the limelight, and without any expectations. A combination of theory and practice had convinced me fully about the Sangh's vision. I was eternally ready to argue for it and fight with people, especially with the secular-type Congressis who were around me. After all there were no Muslims to be seen, one had to go far to seek them out.

One day, suddenly, with no effort on my part, my enemy landed up at home. It happened like this. A Class IV employee was transferred to the government-run primary ayurvedic health centre in Sirdiyas. He wore a netted cap, had a beard and wore salwar-kurta. His name was Amir Khan. One look at him and I knew that this person was from the anti-national community I had been hearing and reading about. Such good fortune to have the enemy fall into my lap, just like that. Without ever interacting with him, I began to apply to Amir Khan the things I had learnt from the shakha and the senior bhaisahabs, and sure enough, quickly convinced myself that the infidel matched up to every single idea I had of the enemy.

I had heard countless times that it was because of these mlechha infidels that our Mother India had been split into two. These people don't see Bharat Mata as their mother but as a witch. They celebrate the victory of Pakistan in cricket. They each have four wives and each produces forty children, trying to increase their population and take over what's left of India. They practise no birth control, refuse vasectomies. They even have protection from the law. They don't obey the Supreme Court. In the case of an old woman called Shah Bano, the government changed the law to please them. They get subsidy to go on Haj, when we have to pay taxes on our pilgrimage to Kailash Mansarovar. Their young men pound iron in foundries through the day, and then emerge all dressed up in the evening to seduce our women, our daughters and daughters-in-law. In schools and colleges they trap our Hindu girls into falling in love with them and trick them into eloping. After exploiting them sexually, they sell them into brothels. In their madarsas, they learn not 'a for alif' but 'a for algaav-vad', or separatism. At the root of all extremism you will find these people. They have arms buried under their masjids. Whenever Pakistan attacks us, these people will be ready to turn on us. They eat beef. They are habitually cruel and heartless. They spy for Pakistan. They are not ours, not of our religion nor of our nation.

Hundreds of such beliefs learnt in the shakha had made themselves at home in my mind, so that when I saw a person like Amir Khan I could not but think of him as a terrorist and an anti-national element. I used to wonder why such dreadful people are allowed to remain in the country. Why doesn't the government use the armed forces to drive them away to Pakistan. But I knew also that the ruling Congress was an appeaser of Muslims. How could we expect any better from these Muslim-loving parties? My own home was full of Congressis. Did I come from a family of anti-national traitors, then? Such questions would often arise in my mind, and as they became more insistent, I redoubled my efforts to consolidate Hindu society through my work in the Sangh. I was convinced that only a strong Hindu society could build a strong India. I had but one objective now—come what may, I would build the Hindu Rashtra in India.

13

Towards the Hindu Rashtra

I was promoted in the hierarchy quite soon. In December 1988 I was promoted from chief teacher to karyavah, the highest post in the shakha. These orders were oral, there was nothing in writing. When swayamsevaks themselves got no receipts or identity cards, why should office bearers? I did ask about this though, and was told that the Sangh did not waste time on such bureaucratic niceties.

I showed a lot of interest in learning and understanding more about the Sangh's ideology, and was particular about attending the shakha regularly, perhaps this was why I was chosen for the greater responsibility. Of course, there were no Brahmin swayamsevaks in my village, and the other non-Brahmin swayamsevaks were not as regular as I was. This must also have been a reason behind my promotion.

I was expected to convene the shakha every day on time, to take the flag and bamboo staff with me, hoist the flag, bring it down at the end of the shakha and keep these safely. There was no provision for expenses incurred, and every day for one hour these responsibilities had to be fulfilled. To go from home to the shakha every day, to be there for the duration of one hour without water or any refreshments provided, to conduct all the activities—the manager was expected to do all of this voluntarily at the level of his village or neighbourhood.

As manager, I was also expected to participate in block-level meetings. When I first went to attend the two-day meeting at the tehsil headquarters, I had to carry with me my bedding, ganvesh, lathi and a plate and bowl to eat from. I had to pay my own fare and also the fee for participating in the meeting. I also carried my food for the first night from home. The first day, the whistle rang at dawn, around 5 am. After ablutions, we would recite in melodious concert the dawn prayer in Sanskrit. Then the shakha began in earnest. All day progress reports of the activities of the Sangh were presented. Food, followed by intellectual sessions. We would sit in different smaller groups and seriously discuss the state of the country.

At the block level meetings, we discussed how to expand membership of the shakhas and to increase the number of shakhas, how to rouse Hindu society, how to make shakhas more valuable in content, and also learnt by heart the chants of the Ekatmata mantra, a mantra of unity that cleverly folds together the sects of the Shaivites, Vaishnavites, Buddhists and Sikhs, under one Brahma, one code of devotion to teachers and parents; and the Bhojan mantra, in praise of food. Much emphasis was placed on physical activity, for the swayamsevak had to be physically strong to fight the enemies of the nation. We were trained in the art of delivering lectures, and given information about the injustices meted out to Hindus. We were given tips on running the ideal shakha, and on how to be the ideal swayamsevak. These two days of collective activity convinced me that the nation-building mission of the Sangh was not human but divine. The opportunity to work with the Sangh came infrequently and only to very fortunate people. It was not a mere organisation, it was a factory that built individuals like me into cultured and patriotic young men.

The pracharak who had come from the district headquarters and the sanghchalak were very inspiring in their speeches. Every sentence they uttered seemed to me like it had come straight from the *Vedas*. Such noble and sage-like people who had dedicated their lives to the nation. I took a mental oath that I too would spend my life trying to achieve the pure goals of the Sangh, that I would be a life-long pracharak.

14

'We want pracharaks, not vicharaks'

Some time after returning from karseva, around May or June 1990, I expressed to the district pracharak, Shiv-ji bhaisahab from Jodhpur, my desire to become a full-time pracharak, giving up family and home, leading the life of an ascetic dedicated to the nation. He gave me a very long reply, of which two things he said are engraved in my memory.

> ME: Bhaisahab, I want to become a pracharak.
>
> DISTRICT PRACHARAK: Brother, your ideals are indeed very high-minded. But you have to see the broader picture. It's all very well that you're excited about becoming a pracharak, but our society is very complicated. Tomorrow, someone asks you your name, your village, your samaj [he said community, but meant my caste], and the moment he realises that pracharak-ji is from a marginalised community, his attitude to you might change. You would have to swallow the insult. I can see this and it's why I'm telling you. You will be upset, want to retaliate. Arguments will follow. All this will weaken the work of the Sangh,

not strengthen it. My advice is to remain a vistarak for a while and serve the nation in that capacity.

I was devastated by his reply. I felt intense pain at having been born in a lower caste community. But how was this my fault? What a predicament for me—here I was, ready to sacrifice my life for the sacred work of the Sangh, but my caste over which I had no control was proving an obstacle. I gradually came around to accepting it, consoling myself that while Hindu society was not yet ready to accept me, the Sangh was relentless in its attempts to bring about the transformation that would end all hierarchy. Soon the time would come when even one such as I, from a lower caste, would be able to work full-time for the nation as a pracharak.

Meanwhile, even before this conversation, I had begun to write. At first there were fiercely nationalist poems. I also brought out an issue of the handwritten magazine *Hindu Kesari*, titled "Annihilate Pakistan". I then began to write columns on nationalist thought in local newspapers. I would go to shakhas in my ganvesh and conduct the intellectual sessions. I lost no opportunity to build myself up as a Hinduvaadi, champion of the Hindu cause. But somehow I felt I was not being accepted the way I wanted to be, as was my right, given all my work.

In the conversation about becoming a pracharak, another thing was said that really showed me my place. Mocking my intellectual work, pracharak-ji indicated my head and said, 'You people who think too much, you're just strong above the neck, not physically. In any case, what the Sangh needs is a pracharak who can convey the message from Nagpur exactly as it was intended, to Hindu society. We don't really want people like you, vicharaks who are constantly questioning and thinking.' And thus my thinking (vichar) made me unfit for the job of propagating the thought of the Sangh (prachar).

You have to understand that the system of pracharaks is the very spine of the Sangh, these are men who have sacrificed everything, all family life, for the cause. One RSS leaflet I consulted states that there are 2,559 pracharaks, of whom 1,646 are for shakha work, 147 for organisational work, 437 for work in Sangh-related bodies, and 335 vistaraks for starting work in new areas. Such figures are released from time to time by the RSS, but they keep changing, because new pracharaks join, others pass away; vistaraks are appointed for limited periods, some of them return home, and so on. The RSS does not make public any consolidated figures about its pracharaks and vistaraks, although scattered information reaches the media on and off.

15

Ideology will be corrupted in Ambedkar hostels

My journey with the Sangh that began in the village, went up the tehsil headquarters, then to the district level at Bhilwara. In Bhilwara town, I stayed in the Ambedkar Hostel run by the social welfare department for students. It was 1991, the centenary of Ambedkar's birth. I was then 16 years old, studying in class eleven. There too I used to sing the praises of the RSS. Since I was seen stepping out in my shorts every evening for the shakha meeting, some seniors used to tease me calling me 'Chadda sahab', punning on chaddi which meant underwear, while Chadda is of course an actual Punjabi surname. But I was so sure of my superiority by now that everyone else appeared far inferior. I used to think, these fools don't know what significant, sacred work I am doing. The day they understand it, they will fall at my feet. I was in a sort of trance of my own. To the other Dalit and Adivasi boys in the hostel, I would talk about Hindutva ideology. Some of my friends in the hostel were Suresh Nakwal, Gopal Nayak, Pyarelal Khoiwal, Bhajjaram Salvi, Ashok Meena, Dayaram Balai, Shyamlal Nayak, Gopal Regar and Ramesh Meena. I even managed to take some of them to the shakha, but they soon dropped off. They didn't like the dress of the Sangh, nor its ways of functioning. I think Ramesh Meena did become a BJP leader, but I don't hear of his being very active these days.

The Ambedkar Hostels were in terrible shape. I stayed in the hostel at Azad Nagar, but the daily routine involved a lot of running around. The toilets were at a distance, and we had to carry our lotas with us; our classes were in another neighbourhood, at the Government Senior Secondary School in Pratapnagar, and for meals we had to go two kilometres away twice a day, to a hostel at Gandhi Nagar. It was exhausting. The Gandhi Nagar hostel was another dilapidated, filthy building like a chicken coop, constructed for students of Scheduled Castes and Tribes. We met at meals at which we were given a limited number of burnt rotis, for which we had to fight like dogs. Dal was basically just water with some spices. Had we taken a dive into it we would not have found even one grain of dal! To this day I loathe dal. There was no attempt at maintaining rules or discipline. Many students chewed tobacco. They got into abusive brawls daily. The hostel warden hardly ever made an appearance. There was nobody to maintain order, no atmosphere for studies. The hostels have now improved somewhat, but those days they were a mess.

The one good thing about our hostel was that everybody was from the Scheduled Castes and Tribes, and so unlike everywhere else, there was no sense of being inferior to anyone. We felt at ease among one another in a way that we never felt anywhere else.

Around this time, the pracharak of Bhilwara town visited

our hostel. I could hardly believe it, but he did come. Having made his own assessment of the students there, he took me aside and said, 'You shouldn't be staying here. This Ambedkar Hostel will corrupt your ideology.'

To protect my ideology, I left the Ambedkar Hostel and reached the district office of the Sangh, where I lived till May–June 1990 along with some other workers. I was given the responsibility of being the pramukh or chief of the district office. I became even more convinced of my capabilities and excellence. I was extremely proud of being a Hindu, and considered myself blessed. Why ever not, when I knew from the core of my being that we Hindus had taught the world what civilisation is. We developed numerals, the decimal. The divinity of our *Vedas* dwarfs the other religious texts of the world. In our land all creatures are considered sacred and women worshipped. The sublime experience of being part of such a civilisation! Slogans such as *Hindi-Hindu-Hindustan, maang raha hai sakal jahan*, Hindi-Hindu-Hindustan, rightfully demands the entire world—the very idea filled me with joy.

So saturated was I with the beliefs of the Sangh that there was no room for other thoughts. I was proud of the *Manusmriti* but that there was such a thing as the Constitution, I had no idea at all. I sang the praises of Maharana Pratap but had never heard of Bhilu Rana Punja. I knew the songs of Mira but was not acquainted with Sant Ravidas. I thrilled to the courage and valour of Rani Lakshmibai of Jhansi, but Jhalkari Bai, a Dalit warrior who played a key role in the Rani of Jhansi's women's army in the 1857 rebellion, was unknown to me. All of the latter were lower castes and Adivasis. If I knew anything about communities like mine, it was about those who had loyally served upper caste idols—Shabari who fed Shri Ram with berries she innocently first tasted herself; of Ekalavya who gave up his thumb as offering to his guru Dronacharya; Hanuman who tore open his chest to reveal Shri Ram enshrined in his heart. The dhobis made themselves useful by washing clothes, leather workers made shoes, others cleaned up after the higher orders; that is, the same ancient caste system and traditional, inherited menial work.

My idols in those days were not Ambedkar, Phule, Kabir, Buddha. I hadn't even heard of them. I knew only Savarkar, Moonje, Tilak, Gokhale, Hedgewar and Guru-ji Golwalkar. They were my inspiration. Pracharak-ji was right. Had I stayed on in the Ambedkar Hostel, my thoughts would have indeed become corrupted.

16

The Sangh, Rajneesh and I

The process of shaking the foundations of my ideological beliefs began with my moving into the Sangh office. One day the nagar pracharak, city disseminator, Kamlesh Chaurasiya, took me to the home of a swayamsevak called Tirath Das. He had recently come under the influence of Osho Rajneesh and had begun to show a lack of interest in the work of the Sangh. We had gone to persuade Tirath Das to return to the right path. We felt he had lost his moorings. Pracharak-ji spoke to him for a long time, but he was adamant. As we left, he gave us a newspaper called *Osho Times*, brought out by Rajneesh's ashram. Pracharak-ji refused to touch it, but I brought it back with me and began to read it. Pracharak-ji couldn't bear it, he snatched it out of my hands, saying, this man will lead you up the wrong path, he will confuse you, never read him. I was stunned and stayed silent, but wondered, how can reading something confuse me? This kindled my interest in Osho and I read the issue of *Osho Times* in secret, which began to open other windows in my mind.

After this, I began to buy *Osho Times* regularly from a bookstall at the Roadways bus-stand of Bhilwara. Later I became friends with a Divakar Java, who lent me his copies of Osho books. Divakar was a Sanghi, part of the Gayatri Parivar, but he was a kind of dissatisfied Sanghi. He read a lot, and along with Osho, he introduced me to Shriram Sharma Acharya, the founder of the All World Gayatri Parivar, headquartered in Haridwar, and to their monthly publication, *Akhand Jyoti*, brought out from their spiritual centre, Shantikunj. However, I found the language of *Akhand Jyoti* dull and off-putting, and used to return it to him mostly unread.

In the RSS I had been trained to value nothing but nationalism, nobility of character, celibacy, spirituality. The relationship between swayamsevaks was seen as pure, other-worldly. To be honest, I had no idea there could be anything like sexual attraction between men, and there were no girls in the shakha anyway. I had come to feel that sex was in fact destructive of the spiritual power of a man. I was full of notions about chastity, especially of women, and the need for women in particular to be good, self-sacrificing wives and mothers. But reading Osho opened my mind to the idea that sexual desire is natural and good.

The sacred and pure ideology of the Sangh that had filled me did begin to be corrupted after all.

17

Is Gulmandi in Pakistan?

Even though my hopes of becoming a pracharak had been dashed, and I had started reading Osho a little, my love for the Sangh, nation-building and Hindutva remained resolute. After leaving the Ambedkar Hostel and moving to the Sangh headquarters, I continued to work as a dutiful swayamsevak. My mind had not opened up enough to consider any alternative, so I worked day and night to build the Hindu Rashtra.

Although the first karseva campaign for Ayodhya had failed, the demand to build the Ram temple was kept on the boil in the Hindu community all over the country. Sangh-affiliated organisations were running a campaign targeting the government with the challenge, 'Build the Ram temple or resign'. On 12 March 1991, we launched a huge rally for the temple at Ayodhya, starting at Sanganeri Gate in Bhilwara and planning to wind through the Muslim majority area of Gulmandi to reach the district collector's office. Thousands of excited young devotees of Ram were waiting outside Doodhadhari temple, saffron bands tied across their foreheads, chanting: *In the name of Ram we swear/ We will build the temple right there.* The government of Rajasthan was BJP. Bhairon

Singh Shekhawat was the chief minister and Banshilal Patwa the MLA from Bhilwara. Meaning, the government was ours. But there the police were, blocking us. Our rally was not being allowed to proceed.

It was a Tuesday. The police thought there might be law and order issues arising from our rally being held at the same time as the afternoon namaz, and was trying to persuade us to follow a different route. They had confidential reports that said there was a possibility of violence being set off between the communities. But the administration was the Sangh's, so we were unafraid. The police were mild and practically pleading before our senior leaders, who refused to relent. Why should our rally not go through Gulmandi? Is Gulmandi in Pakistan? We were adamant that the rally would go through Gulmandi, regardless of consequences.

Even as the confrontation between the police and the Ram-bhakts was on, stones started flying from behind us. The police started a lathi charge. More police, mounted on horses, drove into us, and many were injured. The situation turned more uncontrollable. The police fired in the air, several rounds, and two people were martyred for our cause—Ratanlal Sen from Khamor and Suresh Jain from Bhilwara.

Jain and Sen. Well, the truth is their deaths had nothing to do with Ramjanmabhoomi or our movement to build a Ram temple there. Suresh Jain, a resident of Bhilwara, had returned from night duty and was resting at home. Hearing the commotion, he stepped outside his house to see what was going on, and went down to a police bullet. Ratanlal

Sen of Khamor village was visiting Bhilwara and doing some shopping in the market when he got caught up in the stampede and another police bullet got him. Since both happened to be Hindu—legally, a Jain is regarded as a Hindu in India—they were declared as martyrs for Ramjanmabhoomi, and a protest procession carrying their ashes was promptly announced.

Neither had anything to do with the Sangh or the movement, they were just unfortunate enough to get in the way of police firing. Good for them they were Hindus. They received the title of martyrs. Had they been Muslim, they would have been quietly buried by their families.

18

The police leapt on us with lathis

I was of course part of this rally, somewhere towards the front too. For a while I also threw stones, but as the crowd around me started thinning, I realised I was the only one doing so. I was now worried that I might be hit by lathis or get shot at. Looking around desperately, I spotted Bhimganj School. I ran into it and hid among the students. For a long time we could hear the firing outside. Soon we came to know that curfew had been declared. How was I to leave? It would be impossible. The comforting thought then occurred to me that these students have to be taken home at some point. I could go with them.

The moment things calmed down, arrangements were made to take the children home safely under heavy police security. The police and teachers started taking the students out, and I slipped out with them, but the moment I reached the lane, some five or six policemen burst upon me with lathis. I was wondering how they distinguished me from the other students. Like them, I was young, thin. How did they know I was one of the activists, not a student? I had forgotten the tilak on my forehead and the saffron band around my head. A shower of blows descended on me. I set off running, falling, picking myself up, blubbering in pain, behind me innumerable policemen, their lathis falling on me again and again. Somehow I finally escaped them, and running through Manikyanagar, reached the Mahatma Gandhi Hospital, where thousands of enraged people had gathered. The bodies of the two people killed in police firing had reached there. There were many others who were wounded. I too was bleeding badly, and was given first aid. Then I was taken to the Sangh office. For the next five days of curfew, my poor beaten back was massaged. The mahant of Panchmukhi Balaji temple of RIICO area, Baba Premdas Maharaj, was with us, and others too. Somehow those difficult days passed. As the painkillers started to take effect, I began missing home, and returned to Sirdiyas. But these experiences had affected me badly. I began to feel that one of these days I would be killed either by the police or the infidels. Despite the anxiety, my devotion and dedication to the Sangh never wavered. So convinced was I that the work of the Sangh was work for god that I could not tolerate a word of criticism against the Sangh.

My father was a hard-core Congress supporter, and would often stop me as I set out in my khakhi shorts and black cap, saying, 'This party of Banias and Brahmins will never be with us farmers and lower castes, they just use us to start fights with our miyan brothers, the Muslims. They themselves can never fight, the cowards. They use us.'

My father's words had the nasty smell of Congressi conspiracies. I felt that he too was trapped in the petty politics of caste and Muslim appeasement. Obviously he had no idea of nationalism, or else would he say such things about an organisation dedicated to the service of the nation? I just ignored him as he expressed his disapproval at every stage, from my first stepping out in the RSS uniform, to running away to Ayodhya, or returning beaten from the district headquarters.

He was opposed to my going to the shakha in the first place. When he was really angry, he would hurl abuse at me and the Sangh. It really bugged me. I wanted to say abuse me if you want, but leave the Sangh alone. Not that I ever had the courage to actually say it. I would just feel irritated within. He wanted me to study or help in the fields, but I used to think, me, work in the fields? Here I am, a swayamsevak with such a proud organisation as the Sangh, involved in nothing less than nation-building, and he wants me to leave this factory that constructs human beings, and wander about with him grazing cattle? For me, with my potential to become a pracharak, to be a cowherd? Never. This will never be. I had taken a decision that my work for the Sangh would be for the rest of my life. The most honourable Dr Keshav Baliram Hedgewar-ji had said, 'Nobody ever *was* a swayamsevak of the Sangh. Whether he still works for the Sangh or not, he remains a swayamsevak.'

I was determined that I would not only remain a swayamsevak but be an active one. Whatever my father and my family felt or thought, I didn't care. In any case those Congressis would never understand the divine work of the Sangh, they were just not capable of it. The relationship between my father and I was becoming like the relationship between the Sangh and the Congress. He continued to warn and try to stop me, and I became all the more obstinate about my ideals.

19

When the martyrs' ashes reached my village

Those who had died on the way to Ayodhya and the two men who died in Bhilwara had been declared martyrs. The pots containing their ashes were being paraded from village to village, in asthi kalash (funerary urn) processions with sadhus and sants, Sangh and VHP activists and office bearers. The asthi kalash yatra reached Sirdiyas too, around nine at night, and we received it with due deference. We had decorated our neighbourhood with flowers and leaves, and greeted the procession with the sounds of the conch shell and drums, in a celebration of a kind never seen before.

In April–May 1991, a film was screened at one of our meetings about police brutality towards karsevaks by Mullayam Singh's government at Ayodhya, Ram's birthplace; and the sants and other Hindu leaders described the atrocities in Bhilwara at the hands of the police. Not one of the speakers had been anywhere on the scene or received even a scratch, but the way they described what happened brought tears to everyone's eyes. Although I myself had been injured in Bhilwara, I could not have described the events so movingly. Maybe this is the training we receive from the Sangh. The educated learn very quickly. In any case in our country, those who speak best about hunger are not the hungry but those whose stomachs are full. This was what was happening here. Moving speeches, slogans of *All Hindus are brothers*. Fierce attacks on the inequalities and corruption in Hindu society. The meeting ended with exhortations to Hindus to be united and organised, to embrace the marginalised sections among Hindus. This was the first successful meeting of the Sangh in our Dalit basti.

After it was over, I had arranged for everyone to have a meal at our home. We had prepared poori and kheer for everybody. As the preparations for the meal were under way, my father again tried to stop me, 'Why are you wasting food? These people will not eat with us. Hypocrites, they say one thing in public, but do something else. They are filled with poison against us.' I was furious. I gathered up all my courage to contradict him sharply, 'What do you know about the Sangh? I have been with them for five years. I am the chief of the district office. I have eaten at so many swayamsevaks' homes. The Sangh is not like your village, with untouchability and caste prejudice. That's the kind of thing the Congress has given us.' My father said, 'Son, the Congress is like the mother's womb for our caste. You just don't understand. But fine, it's a great thing if there is no caste discrimination in your organisation. Make the food, I am only too happy to feed everyone.'

So there was a kind of ceasefire between us. I was amenable, and he wasn't angry. The food was ready, and soon those who were to partake of it would be here too.

I was rushing around making arrangements in an exultant mood. For the first and perhaps the last time in my life, I had actually sung and danced in the procession. I had conducted the proceedings also. I had never been so happy and excited in my life. I felt as if it was not the devotees of Ram but the deity himself who was coming to my home, just as he had gone to Sabari's humble hut. I was also thrilled to be able to prove my Congressi father wrong; in his Congress dominated village I had established the flag of Hindutva. The day's successful programme was a step in the direction of the Hindu Rashtra. Just that morning I had put up two stickers on our front door: *Garv se kaho hum Hindu hain*, Say it with pride, we are Hindu; and *Bade bhagya se hum Hindu hain*, We are blessed to be Hindu.

20

Friend, pack up the food

The moment I invited the participants to come home for a meal, there was a sudden hesitation. The acting district chief of Seva Bharti was an office bearer of the Sangh and he took me aside. His name was Nandlal Kast, of about fifty years of age, a Bania. He had been an office-holder in the Sangh for around twenty years and ran a Sanghi school. Affectionately placing his hand on my shoulder, he showered me with praise for my organisation of the day's event. This went on for a while, gradually changing register to a larger appreciation of my work for the Sangh and for the Nation, until finally in a very low voice, he said, 'Friend, you are aware of the inequalities in our society. Despite all the efforts of the Sangh, Hindu society has not become one. As far as we ourselves are concerned, we would sit down with you any day and eat from the same plate, but today there are sadhu–sants and others also here. They will be really upset if without informing them, we give them food from a lower caste home. They could be so angry they might leave.'

His words turned me to stone. Had you cut me, I would not have bled. My mind was buffeted by a storm of thoughts.

No words would come to my tongue. Once I understood what he was saying, I couldn't even listen to him further as he went on and on. But the last thing he said I remember to this day. 'Why don't you pack the food and have it put in the car. We will feed them all in the next village.'

Of course his meaning was crystal clear. Keeping it a secret that the food was from a Dalit swayamsevak's home, everyone would be quietly fed.

I felt defeated in my own home. But I didn't know by whom. My father had won, but it was the Sangh that had struck the blow. What would I tell father if he asked why they wouldn't eat in our house? Still, I hardened my heart and started packing the food up. When my family asked why, I replied 'They are already running late for the next programme in Bhagwanpura village, so they will eat there.' I managed to get them off my back, but my joy had fled. I experienced fully what it meant to be of a lower caste. Again and again the thought troubled me: How can this happen? How can the Sangh do this to me? They don't believe in untouchability, in caste discrimination, they believe all Hindus to be one, they talk of a united Hindu society, and then this kind of hypocrisy?

I thought, here I am, a disciplined swayamsevak, a passionate swayamsevak, a district office chief. If this can happen to me, what kind of intolerable behaviour must the rest of my community face? For the first time in my life that day, I stepped aside from my Hindu identity and started seeing the world like a person from a lower caste. My troubled thoughts kept me awake all night, a night that felt endless. Little did I know that the morning's sun would arise on a still bleaker day.

The next day was like apocalypse. The night of the knives had barely passed when the sun appeared with a glaring face. My friend Purushottam Shrotriya, a Brahmin who had gone with the asthi kalash yatra, came back to Sirdiyas. I knew him from my Ambedkar Hostel days, and we were good friends due to our interest in poetry. We used to attend the Azad Nagar shakha together. We shared everything. Our friendship was deep.

When he returned in the morning, he was carrying the kettle in which the kheer had been sent. The story he told me was inconceivable and beyond belief. It came like hammer blows to my skull. Purushottam said that the food I had sent was thrown out on the road just before Bhagwanpura, and the night's meal was provided from the home of a Brahmin, Ramswaroop Sharma, very late at night. Purushottam had been told not to tell me, but he couldn't bring himself to lie. 'Your food was not eaten, it was thrown away,' he said. I just couldn't believe it. I said to him, you must be joking, our people in the Sangh can't possibly be so casteist and cruel. He said if you don't believe me, come and see for yourself, some of it must still be lying there. We set off on cycles towards Bhagwanpura, and I saw with my own eyes, there on the side of the road, the food I had sent from home, lying scattered about. And crows, kites, ants and dogs, with no discrimination amongst themselves, were feeding on it.

My heart was broken.

The asthi kalash yatra was to reach the Brahmin village of Sareri that evening. I decided to go there and confront them. Enough. Time for the decisive battle. The fighting had begun, though war was yet to be declared.

21

Nobody, nowhere ready to listen

I reached the Brahmin village Sareri in the evening, full of rage. I demanded an explanation for the shameful conduct of the participants in the yatra. But they flatly denied throwing away the food. When I told them I had got the information straight from Purushottam-ji, they changed their tune and said, oh yes, as the car turned the corner towards Bhagwanpura at high speed, the food flew out of the hands of the person holding it. Between their words and their looks, the truth was clear to me. I thought, how easily these Most Revered Bhaisahabs can lie. I was convinced they were lying through their teeth. If the food had flown out of someone's hands, it would have fallen in the middle of the road, how did it reach the side? And second, the pooris could have fallen in the mud, but at least the kheer in the kettle would have been safe, and in any case, if the kettle too had fallen, it would have been scratched and dented, which it wasn't.

There could be no doubt. They had deliberately thrown away food prepared in a Dalit swayamsevak's home, and when confronted, instead of accepting their fault, they were coming up with strange and incredible explanations. Their lies and their attempts to present their lie as truth broke my heart. I felt intense humiliation and a sense of insult, as if the Sangh had not only rejected the food from my home, but that it was me that they had picked up and thrown far away. I felt utterly distant from them, they were liars and hypocrites.

My years of work with the Sangh passed before me like a film. How I had put in all my strength towards fulfilling its goals, how I had run away from home to become a martyr for Shri Ram. Had I reached Ayodhya, and fallen to police bullets on the bridge over the Sarayu, would these people have even touched my corpse? Would it be conveyed to my family, or, like the unwanted food from my home, would it be thrown into the Sarayu? I asked myself, was it for this Hindu Rashtra I was working so hard, so ready to kill and be killed? There is no place for me here at all. What is my own identity? What am I? Who am I after all? A devotee of Ram, a Hindu karsevak, or a Shudra, an untouchable? One so impure that even the food from my home could not be touched by these flag-bearers of Hindu Rashtra! What was my identity?

Later, I realised that in the Hindu caste system, I was lower than the Shudra, I was an untouchable; not one of the four varnas, but an outcaste, the fifth caste, avarna. I may well be a swayamsevak, but I was not a Hindu all the way. This must be why I was unacceptable. Why I was permitted to rise only up to vistarak, and discouraged from becoming a pracharak. I said to myself—enough. Now I have to know myself. I have to search out the reasons for these things that have happened to me, and exterminate their roots. I decided to take my principled objections to this discrimination and injustice all the way to Nagpur, to the Sangh headquarters. I spoke to as many influential people as I could, from leaders in the asthi kalash yatra to pracharaks at different levels. There was nobody with whom I did not share my pain, no level I didn't approach, but when I saw that I was not getting a hearing anywhere, I took my cry for help up to the sarsanghchalak, Balasaheb Deoras, himself. I wrote to him, told him the whole story, said that your local leaders don't want me to stay a Hindu and carry on my work with the Sangh for a day longer.

But who was I, an insignificant being, to be heard in the corridors of power? No response from there either. Of course, this was not surprising. Every person I spoke to dismissed my complaint as a small matter, and in fact it was I who was given advice. Give up all this negativity, get on with doing positive work. But I just couldn't accept that this was a small matter. Not then, and not today. Untouchability and discrimination is not a small matter in anybody's life. To declare someone untouchable by birth and then refuse to accept their hospitality—this can be a small matter only for the architects of the Hindu Rashtra; in my life it was huge.

22

Thoughts of ending my life

I received no reply to the letter I wrote to the sarsanghchalak. I kept up my questioning, I kept arguing at every level, but at every level there was a strange silence. I was to meet with disappointment everywhere. Not a single person was willing to see the seriousness of the incident, to them it seemed trivial. After all, these things happen in our society, what's the big deal, why was I getting so worked up about it. Meanwhile, I was going through pain the likes of which I had never experienced before. Utterly confused about what to do. Unable to think, unable to act. Sinking into despondency. Nobody gave a thought to the agony eating away at me. The world went its way, uncaring, and I started to think, why should I continue living? I started to think about suicide, of the many ways I could carry it out. Hang myself, jump into a well, take poison and free myself forever. I came to the conclusion that poison was the best way. There was rat poison at home.

One night I ate the poison along with my food. I went to bed thinking there would never be another morning in my life. I think I fell asleep soon after, but a half-awake kind of sleep. I was alive, but also dying. A powerful wave of pain arose in my stomach. Nausea overwhelmed me. The pain was unbearable, I ran outside to vomit. As I vomited violently, it was as if my liver had reached my mouth, my insides were pouring out, my head spun, my consciousness started to fade away.

By now my panicking family had realised I was very ill, and my elder brother Badri-ji was informed. He rushed to me, reaching just as my eyes were closing. He asked me what had happened, and I was able to say before passing out—I took rat poison. Later I was told that my brother ran to get the doctor, and Dr Suresh Chandra Sharma reached very quickly. He gave me several injections of glucose, and started treating me. So that the police should not come to know, everything was done in secret. Bhaisahab was so caring, he did not speak about this at all to anyone. I was saved because of his immediate action and that of Dr Sharma. Badri bhaisahab was very angry with the RSS when he came to know the reason for my attempt at suicide, but in time he cared less about it, and in fact eventually forgot the incident altogether.

At the time, although Badri bhaisahab was careful, Dr Sharma was indiscreet, and the news spread like fire through the village. I recovered my health, but was filled with shame and sadness. It seemed I could succeed at nothing, not even at taking my life. Life won, and death lost. I felt as if every person in Sirdiyas knew about my idiocy, and out of a sense of humiliation, I did not meet anyone for months. In order to escape it all, I went to Bhilwara.

Once I reached the town, I started to question myself. Why was I ready to die, and for whom? For what? Would anybody care if I died? When I contemplated my own foolishness, I wanted to hit myself on the head in frustration. I was ready to die in Ayodhya out of love for them; and I was ready to die again because of their hateful behaviour. In either case, it was I who was to die. Sometimes in joy, sometimes in sorrow—were they the masters of my life? Was the Sangh's love or hatred something to live or die for? Why should I die? Why do I need their certificate, who the hell are they to decide the course of my thinking, my life? Why am I still with them? Why am I working with such petty, mean-minded, hypocritical people? Why am I working towards a Hindu Rashtra that will discriminate against me? Hundreds of such sharp and bitter questions overwhelmed me. After much inner churning and deep thought that brought me almost to the point of exhaustion, I decided not only to make a clean break with the Sangh, but that I would widely publicise their casteist behaviour towards me. It would be my life's work now to expose the reality of this dishonest Hindutva and its dreams of a Hindu Rashtra. I resolved to tear the veil of fake harmony from the face of the Sangh and its family of institutions and expose their real face in public. Knowing full well how limited my resources were, I was determined to apply all my strength, and set out by myself to fight the massive organisation of the Sangh. This struggle would be life-long, until my last breath.

23

And when Babri was brought down

May 1991 marked the beginning of my days of struggle. It was an endless battle, fought on many fronts, with myself and with the world at large. I continued to rest my hopes in the RSS, believed that I would somehow get justice. I met anyone who would listen, poured out my woes, but nothing came of it. During this time, I met other swayamsevaks, office-bearers and pracharaks, and presented my case. Their only counsel to me was to keep up a positive outlook. Not one of them thought the matter of caste discrimination and untouchability to be an issue at all, for them it was all very commonplace and not worth discussing.

The period between May 1991 and December 1992 was one of utter despair. Living in the village didn't give me peace, and in Bhilwara I had no place to stay. I roamed aimlessly, sometimes with nowhere to spend the night. Like the homeless I slept in parks, the very parks where I once stalked around proudly in my Sanghi garb. Food was hard to come by. With no money, I spent entire days without a bite of a roti. I'd land up at the homes of relatives and acquaintances at meal times. Or, I showed up at the Ambedkar Hostel where I found both food and a place to sleep.

The mass fervour for karseva and the demolition of Babri Masjid came back with a vengeance in 1992. But this time my destination was not Ayodhya. The battle now was for my self-respect. In the relentless pursuit of equality and justice that I was now engaged in, Babri was no longer an issue. Those headed to Ayodhya, I felt, were utterly misguided. This time, no one from my family or village joined the karseva. I made it a point to speak to many people, especially those who belonged to Scheduled Castes, telling them about my experience with the RSS to try and stop them from throwing their lot with these hypocrites.

But I was alone, so my efforts were not that successful. Those who wished to go, went anyway. Not me though. I was not intoxicated by devotion to Ram this time, I felt lost, indifferent to everything, distant from all that was unfolding, like it had nothing to do with me.

Around then, I also began work with some friends to establish a students' outfit (that eventually became Vidyarthi Adhikar Rakshak Sangh or VARS). For some time, I settled into a temple off the Krishi Upaj Mandi (a state-run farmers' market) in Bhilwara, only to move out soon enough. My belongings were scattered across the different places I haunted—in the RSS district office, the temple, the Ambedkar hostel, and Sitaram Dharamshala, a choultry. At every place that I was forced to leave, I left something behind. With the exception of Ambedkar Hostel, I never returned to any of these places.

On the evening of 5 December, I went to meet students

at the Ambedkar Hostel. By 1991, the hostel had shifted from its rented premises in Azad Nagar to a permanent building in Bapu Nagar. I was at the hostel on 6 December when we heard the news of the demolition of Babri Masjid on the radio. We did not respond to it in any way, or discuss it among ourselves. I just left, took an auto and headed to the Bhilwara market where I saw jubilant Hindus bursting crackers and distributing sweets. By contrast, there was visible police bandobast at the mosque near the railway station. The Muslim majority areas were marked by such massive police presence that it was as if curfew had been clamped, an eerie silence reigned. Worried that the situation could get out of hand, and that I may be trapped in the town, I left that night around 10 pm for my home in Sirdiyas. There, I slept through the night.

In a few days I learnt that restrictions had been placed on the RSS for its role in bringing down the Babri Masjid. There had been a raid at the RSS office in Bhilwara, located above the Bajrang Daal Baati Bhojanalaya (Bajrang Lunch Home), and documents had been seized. The key office bearers of the RSS, fearing arrest, went underground. When I came to know from the Maandal police that my name also figured in the documents, I too went into hiding as a precaution. But the truth is that the police were never serious about apprehending anyone. They could have easily arrested me if they wanted to. The raids had all been a big charade.

At home of course, the demolition of Babri Masjid did come up for discussion. While my mother was just relieved that her sons had not been involved this time, my father felt that what these people had done was not right. A house of god had been destroyed. He would say again and again, these Janata Party people (as he called them; these days he says BJP) are only making us fight with each other for votes.

The Ramjanmabhoomi for which I took part in the 1990 karseva, for which I suffered police brutality, went to jail, was ready to die for; the mosque I was so eager to bring down and the Ram temple for which I was willing to take lives—when all these impulses finally reached their conclusion, I felt no joy. There was neither a sense of victory nor defeat. The Ram temple simply did not figure in my priorities any longer. Perhaps I had realised that it was all just an excuse to humiliate the Muslims, something I too had been enthusiastic about earlier. But this time, even before Babri fell, I had fallen quite low myself.

24

When we took on the ABVP

I was by now well equipped to hit the Indian version of the Taliban where it hurt. I started off by entering student politics. In 1993, I enrolled for a Bachelor of Arts degree in Manikyalal Verma Government College in Bhilwara where the RSS student wing, the Akhil Bharatiya Vidyarthi Parishad (ABVP), was dominant. The same year, a new student organisation called Vidyarthi Adhikar Rakshak Sangh or VARS—Organisation for the Protection of Students' Rights—was started in opposition to the ABVP. It was was headed by another rebel swayamsevak, Brijraj Krishna Upadhyaya, who broke with the ABVP because he was not given a leadership position. Dhiraj Gujjar and I threw our lot with him. In its inaugural phase I was the general secretary of VARS. We began to pull the rug from under the feet of the Sanghi student organisation. We set up units of VARS in Bhilwara and Shahpura. People who wanted freedom from the stranglehold of the Sangh began to see VARS as an alternative. Our leader Brijraj Krishna was extraordinarily brave, very spirited. The Sangh attacked him ferociously, they could not tolerate his starting a new organisation. He was physically attacked many times by the ABVP, beaten up mercilessly even in public. Once, at the Triveni crossing in Mandalgarh, they attacked him with a screwdriver, drove it into his skull and left him for dead. This last attack was meant to punish him because VARS activists were exposing the criminal activities of people linked to the Sangh.

Those days in Mandalgarh town, a mining area, the short term pracharaks and vistaraks of the Sangh were involved in protection rackets with gangs manufacturing illegal explosives and bootlegged liquor. I had no idea about this when I was in the RSS and it came to my knowledge only when I left the organisation. We learnt that some respectable bhaisahabs of the Sangh were also extorting money from these gangs. Because we raised these matters in public, we had to pay the price. VARS as an organisation became the target of attack, but Brijraj Krishna bore the brunt of it, and received such beatings that he was almost martyred at the hands of Sanghi swayamsevaks. Mandalgarh is a sandmining region, and the mining mafia thinks nothing of killing anyone who gets in their way. The intention was to murder Upadhyaya at the Triveni crossing, but passers-by got him, gravely wounded as he was, to Mahatma Gandhi Hospital in Bhilwara in time. After a lengthy period of treatment, he did recover.

I remained friends with him for a long time, and we continued to work in student politics. Eventually he moved into the arena of state elections and contested as an independent for the legislative assembly. He is now active in the Congress, and never returned to the BJP or the RSS.

It was not just a matter of exposing the misdeeds of the Sangh's 'disciplined' swayamsevaks, but to expose the reality of the organisation that constantly talked about good character and culture, but did not hesitate to publicly humiliate a woman office-bearer of their student organisation. How could we remain silent about their fraudulence and hot air about character and culture? When we started to make these things public, they showed up to discuss things with us with their all-too-familiar weapon, the danda or lathi. Most of the time, Sangh activists prefer to use the lathi rather than argument, having been trained to think that blows are more effective than talk. For many years, VARS fought bravely against all attempts by Sangh overlords to turn the university into a battlefield of gangsters, and made its mark in student politics. In many colleges our candidates won elections, not only against the ABVP but also against the NSUI, National Students Union of India of the Congress party. Offering an alternative students' politics, VARS was active for a very long time, raising not only students' issues but also wider political questions, and keeping students away from casteism and communalism. Today I strongly feel the need for such a students' organisation that can battle established gangster politics on campuses.

25

The desire for revenge

I wanted to take revenge on the RSS in whatever way I could, and was ready to join hands with anybody for this. After all, the enemy of an enemy is a friend. So I started to meet with all the people that the RSS had taught me were bad. My circle of acquaintances began to include people from other faiths and secular-minded people too. Earlier, I had known hardly any people of this kind, but I had come across a few Muslims in another context. Those days I used to attend poetry gatherings at which I would recite shoddy satirical verse in Rajasthani. Here I met Jamaluddin 'Jauhar', Aziz 'Zakhmi' and Maulana Naushad Alam. There was also a trade union leader called Allauddin 'Bedil'. They used to recite poetry too, and we often ran into one another at these gatherings.

I decided to deepen my acquaintance with such people. Naushad Alam was about my age, and we used to talk about many things other than literature. So I set off to meet him.

Naushad Alam was from Bihar originally, and lived in Bhagwanpura near my village Sirdiyas, where he was the imam of the mosque and also taught in the madarsa. Writing ghazals was his hobby. Later he went on to become the imam of the Gulnagari mosque in Bhilwara. By then, the second wave of karseva had been completed and the Babri Masjid had been destroyed. Muslims were angry and, especially among Muslim youth, there was intense rage towards the Sangh. It was in these circumstances that I set off to meet Naushad, albeit with some hesitation.

There I was, sitting in a madarsa attached to the mosque. While in the Sangh, I had heard a lot about weapons being stored in the basements of mosques, which made me a little scared, but now that I was here, I was determined to have a conversation. After finishing with his teaching at the madarsa, Naushad went to offer namaz. When he returned, we started talking.

This conversation started to melt the ice of hatred towards Muslims I held in my heart. Those whom I thought dangerous and had been suspicious of, turned out to be people like me. Just like us, in their laughter, their tears, their anger; just as patriotic as us; as beset by difficult circumstances as we are. For the first time in my life I went inside a mosque, sat in a madarsa, saw their kitchen, their bedrooms, sat with them, ate with them. This was the village, Bhagwanpura, where food from my home had been rejected and thrown away, and today in that very village, I sat down to eat with a maulana.

All misunderstandings vanished, and that one meeting—where we primarily discussed poetry and patriotism—built such a strong relationship that it stands firm till today. Our encounter that day and the hours of conversation in the days that followed, ranging from poetry to politics, resulted in the recognition that the condition of Muslims and Dalits was equally bad, that our enemy was the same, and we should fight it together. The decision was taken to form two organisations, one of Dalit youth and another of Muslim youth.

In December 1993, I started the Dalit Action Force and Maulana Naushad started the Hyder-e-karrar Islamic Sevak Sangh. The objective of both was to expose the activities of the RSS and whenever necessary to launch direct campaigns against them. These organisations held discussions in different places and many people began joining in. But before we could really take off, information about our efforts reached the intelligence agencies. This information was available from our own press notes and from an interview with me in *Dahakte Angaarey* (a periodical I started, about which more later). Our mistake in publicising our plans before they could take off taught us that while this may bring publicity, it was not the way to build movements or organisations, because the CID (Criminal Investigation Department) and IB (Intelligence Bureau) joined with the local police in going after us with threats and warnings.

So our two organisations were stillborn. We were helpless. But our failure did not defeat me. Rather, my anger grew.

Naushad's quest eventually led him to the Communist Party of India–Marxist Leninist (CPI-ML), and he served as block president of Salkuan Bazaar in Saharsa district of Bihar for four years. He is now Kosi zone president of the Aam Aadmi Party.

I, for my part, decided that the way to counter the RSS was to convert out of Hinduism.

26

Attempts at religious conversion

I started to think seriously about religious conversion, but to which religion? My experience in the Sangh had taught me that Sikhism, Jainism and Buddhism were part of Hindu society. Islam was out of the question, because I had been fed so much disinformation about its cruelty and violence that I had enormous distrust of it and did not consider it as a possibility. That left Christianity. I thought, why not become a Christian, the Sangh hates them as much as they hate Muslims. But here was the problem—where were Christians to be found? I had never met a Christian, let alone had Christian acquaintances, although I had read a lot about them while in the Sangh. I had also heard that if one became a Christian, one was given a girl and a job, and I didn't want either. I just wanted revenge. I wanted to infuriate those who had insulted and rejected me.

I started searching for Christians. In early 1994, I met the owner of a printing press in Azad Nagar in Bhilwara, whose name was Bethuel Gaekwad. What happened was that my cousin Mangi Devi's husband Chhaganlal, who was a compositor, had recently got a job at this press, and when I landed there to meet him, both my objectives were met. This gentleman, Bethuel, also owned a church and a school. I had a chat with him and, disclosing my agenda, asked, can I become a Christian? He asked me why I wanted to become a Christian, and I told him about my struggle against the RSS and my desire for revenge. But Pastor Gaekwad insisted, 'Christianity believes not in revenge but in forgiveness. So forgive them, come to Church regularly, believe in Jesus. He is our liberator and the answer to all our questions.'

I responded sharply that I was not seeking liberation, nor god. Nor did I have any questions. I wanted no answers. I had one objective and one alone—to expose the hypocrisy of the Sangh and its unethical politics. He listened to me in all seriousness, and invited me to prayer the following Sunday. But before I could participate in the prayer meeting, he sent word to my family through my brother-in-law that I should be counselled as I was trying to become a Christian.

Later I tried other churches—Baptist, Church of North India, Methodist, Syrian, Catholic and countless others. To each I told my story and said make me a Christian, but all of them stepped back, scared when they heard the name RSS. They thought I was a spy for the RSS trying to entrap them, and would hastily send me on my way. I did not succeed in my plan anywhere.

27

Jesus acceptable, but not Christianity

But I am not one to accept defeat. I met a schoolteacher who was originally a Brahmin. He had converted to Christianity and from Harinarayan Joshi, had become H. Newman. He gave me some spiritual instruction. But of course I was not interested in what was being thrust at me. Nor in the Bible, Jesus, church or liberation. My goal was clear to me. Newman left me cold. Understanding this, Newman gave me the address of a Seventh Day Adventist pastor, telling me to write to him, perhaps he could help me. I posted a letter, and within a few days, two unfamiliar men were at my door, asking me for my own address. I told them it was I they were looking for. One of them was the pastor I had written to, Pastor Parvez from Jodhpur. I invited them in, served them tea. They listened to my story and said with smiles, come with us to Jodhpur. The next day I set off. I stayed with Pastor Parvez for three months. He taught me chapter and verse of the Bible, taught me the importance of patience, mercy and repentance. I must have studied enough to get a Bachelor of Theology degree. But the fact was that in thought, word and deed, I was still a rebel Hindu and it was difficult for him to trust me. So one day the congregation of his church and he himself, decided that I should be baptised. For this I had first to present myself before the district collector of Jodhpur and declare that I wanted to convert to Christianity. I flatly refused to do it. All I wanted to do was provoke and anger the RSS, nothing more and nothing less. So they discussed it with one another, gave up the idea of legally converting me, and decided to induct me secretly by the rituals of baptism.

One Sunday they sang some songs, read a few verses from the Bible, dunked me in a tank of water and pulled me out. Then they covered me in white cloth and said in my ear, 'You have been reborn today'. This procedure is called being 'born again'. Now I had become worthy of trust in their eyes. But the hollowness of this religion was clear to me. What sort of religion is it where the answer to every question is Jesus? I began to feel mutinous—what was I allowing to happen to myself? It felt like I had climbed out of a ditch and fallen into a well.

I was not able to suppress this inner rebel. I made it clear to them that I could even accept Jesus, but not this Christianity of theirs. Well may you pray in English, wearing your suit and tie and shoes, but you are no less foolish than the others. I began to find all organised religion repellent, and grew desperate to claw my way out of the dry well of Christianity. Soon I bid them goodbye.

Freedom from them was a relief. I slept easy again, having realised that liberation was to be found, not in the Bible, Jesus or Christianity, nor in any religion, but in liberating myself from all of that. I realised I was not religious, and discovered my happiness in this realisation, that I was not a believer, and did not seek a place in heaven. I was on a train to hell, and couldn't have been happier.

28

What makes them such Brahmins?

Thanks to the Sangh's concern that the Ambedkar Hostel would wreck my ideology, I had left it in December 1990, and by May 1991 my roof at the Sangh office was also gone. I needed a new place to stay. A priest I knew, Sant Chaitanya Sharan Shastri, who claimed to be the personal assistant of Atal Bihari Vajpayee, had taken over a Shiv Hanuman temple in the Krishi Mandi area in Bhilwara. I started living with him. Although he too was a hard-core Hindutvavaadi, he happened to be in a sulk with the Sangh. His status had not been acknowledged adequately during some yatra, a junior priest had been shown more respect, something like that. So the pair of us, disgruntled Hindutvavaadis both, made common cause and started living together.

I kept busy with student politics during the day and reached Shastri-ji's place only at night to rest. Those were very difficult times, often I had not a single paisa and went hungry. There had been days, before I moved in with Shastri-ji, when I spent the whole night out in the park, famished and thirsty. And then there was the pressure of my Angry Young Man persona—whenever I got the opportunity I would speak and write against the RSS. Those days nobody took much notice of me or my ranting, but I kept up my campaign. People saw me as an eternal contrarian and bellyacher. The Sangh, though, ignored me totally. Zero response to anything I said or wrote. Just cold silence. Which riled me further. Shastri-ji would advise me on and off: Don't keep taking on the Sangh like this, you don't know these people yet. They're capable of stuffing you into a sack, pounding you to a pulp, and you wouldn't be able to hear your own crying, forget about the world. I ignored his words.

Chaitanya Sharan Shastri-ji was a good person, but casteist to the bone. One time, we had gone to take our evening meal at a Bihari industrialist's home near a Ganesh temple in Gandhi Nagar. Possibly on account of some religious ritual, his invitation was to Brahmins. And Shastri-ji took me along. I had no idea of the context, I only knew that we were to dine at a rich Bihari Baniya's house. Since spending time with people at their homes and eating with them was a common practice with the Sangh, it did not seem strange to me. As part of the senior Sangh structure myself, I had often gone with pracharaks to dine at swayamsevaks' homes, many of them so-called upper castes. Without any hesitation, I went along with Shastri-ji.

During the meal, the host asked my name, and I answered, Bhanwar Meghwanshi. As they were from Bihar, he and his family were not familiar with the caste system of Rajasthan, and he asked, 'What sort of Brahmins are they?' I opened my mouth to say 'I am from a Scheduled...' but before I could go further, Shastri-ji hastily broke in, 'They are Kshatriya Brahmins'.

The matter ended there, but the indignity of having my caste concealed made the food go bitter in my mouth. Meanwhile Shastri-ji was angry with me for trying to declare my Scheduled Caste status. We argued fiercely later. I accused him of being underhanded in his treatment of people's religious beliefs, and he ended up saying straight out, that I was living proof people of lower castes have lower intelligence. Here I am, trying to make you a Brahmin, he went, and you prefer to crawl about in that dirty gutter.

I was trembling with rage, and wanted to thrash this hypocrite. I didn't, of course, but I matched him abuse for abuse. I yelled, you are no better, a beggar by caste. When have you ever eaten a mouthful earned through your own hard work?

And so Shastri-ji declared me to be a low-caste insect of the gutter and I certified him as a beggar. We could not live together after this. I left the temple. My staying on might have cast a shadow over his Brahmin-ness, maybe even affected his income from conducting rituals.

Besides, staying put implied a submission to Brahminical values, which would weaken my stand against the Sangh. And so we parted ways. I could not become a Brahmin and he was not willing to become human. We never met again.

I was out of the temple and didn't feel like returning home to my parents. Ever since the Sangh had thrown out the food cooked at our place, I had not found the courage to go back. I wandered about in Bhilwara, sleeping here and there, eating when I could. No fixed residence, filled with indecision, not in my right mind. Naturally, my studies were affected.

I had taken admission for an Arts degree at the Manikya Lal Verma Government College, and for a year did student politics there, but could not write the exam. When my father came to know of this, he was very angry and ticked me off severely. I was fortunate he did not beat me.

Anyway, all this affected my education and I was to complete all further studies through correspondence courses and self-learning.

In those difficult days, I was given shelter by Daulat Raj Nagoda in his small room in Gandhi Nagar, Bhilwara. He had also been an RSS swayamsevak, and had received officers' training. He had worked in the Sangh office, and would teach in the Sangh's Adarsh Vidya Mandir school in Badnaur. He was acknowledged to be a very active swayamsevak. His lectures were clear and accessible. He spoke like a teacher, so that anyone could understand. He knew all the Sangh songs by heart and often sang them. These qualities gave him great success in mobilising people.

Despite his undoubted commitment to the Sangh, he too had come through some bitter experiences of discrimination and untouchability.

Once at an RSS Officers' Training Camp held at Maharaja Ajmid Adarsh Vidya Mandir, he insistently raised questions about the steps taken by the Sangh for the abolition of caste, but the Sangh functionaries present refused to engage with him. Finally the senior pracharak said something insulting to Daulat-ji, and the atmosphere turned so heated that they came to blows. Daulat-ji is solidly rustic in his ways, militant and unafraid. There was no question of his retreating. In the presence of hundreds of Sangh activists he tore at pracharak-ji's hair and gave as good as he got. After this he stayed away from the RSS. He formed the Ambedkar Savings Society, a micro-credit and small savings group, that also sought to bring Dalits together, set up legal literacy classes for Dalit and Adivasi youth, and worked relentlessly to draw them into the mission launched by Phule, Kabir and Ambedkar. He is still involved in this campaign.

After leaving the Sangh, Daulat-ji took a room on rent in Gandhi Nagar and joined an electrician's training course at the Industrial Training Institute. These institutes are state run, but even here the Sanghis had a strong presence, and he had to deal with constant harassment. In these tough circumstances he eventually got his degree. He set up a a little kiosk and sold paan to finance his law studies. He then started legal practice, largely assisting the poor and taking on their cases, and till today this is what he does. It was with such a committed comrade that I shared a small room for many days, and that's where I got obsessed with the idea of starting a newspaper. I was searching for some medium of expression through which I could expose the Sangh and its hypocritical ideology. This seed eventually grew to become the fortnightly, *Dahakte Angaarey.*

Daulat Raj Nagoda has been my steadfast companion since then. Many a time, fatwas were issued against us by the hateful forces of the Sangh, we were sharply criticised, countless attempts were made to drive us apart. But despite their best efforts the Sangh could neither separate us from each other, nor the two of us from the oppressed Dalits we sought to work with. Our voices, raised in favour of the oppressed and the marginalised, far from being silenced by the Sangh's attacks, were only strengthened. Today Daulat Raj Nagoda is an established lawyer. He has been elected unopposed three times to the post of chairperson of the Asind Bar Association and is a leading figure in the Dalit movement in Rajasthan.

29

Towards Ambedkarism

I returned to my village in August 1995. Now I was more inclined to make a political response. The Dalit–Muslim alliance had failed to take off, and Christianity turned out to be not at all different from Hinduism. It seemed all religions were equally rigid and irrational. On the surface it was all *sarva dharma sama bhava*—treat all religions equally—but actually every religion had a secret agenda to expand its followers and control the world. Some wanted to make the whole world dar-ul-islam, subject to the laws of Islam; while others were insistent upon sharing the gospel with one and all. As for Hindus, they were no better. Declaring *krinvanto vishvam aryam* ('Let us Aryanise the world', meaning, elevate it), the Rig Vedic verse made popular by Dayanand Saraswati as the motto of the Arya Samaj, they were bent upon 'civilising' the world. Each one expansionist, each conjuring visions of heaven and hell. I wanted to run far away from the abstractions of fear, fortune and god.

So I started searching for alternative writings, and started with Ambedkar's works.

Until now, I knew of Ambedkar in two ways. First was through the RSS, where in every morning prayer at the shakha we remembered Ambedkar. I had also read the Sangh-approved story of his life written by Dattopant Thengadi. Second was through my reading of Osho, where Gandhi was criticised and Ambedkar counterposed to him as the more scientific and rational thinker.

I had read about Babasaheb Ambedkar here and there in Sangh publications like *Panchjanya, Pathey Kan, Rashtra Dharma* and *Jahnavi*, from which I learnt that Babasaheb was a great nationalist, and had contributed to writing the Constitution of India. That he had wanted to make Sanskrit the national language and the saffron flag the national flag. That despite every temptation, he had not converted to Islam or Christianity but to Buddhism, which was part of Hinduism. And that he was opposed to the continuation of Article 370 in Kashmir, which gave the state a special status.

Now I was reading Ambedkar himself, and found that his views on everything were the exact opposite of what the Sangh claimed. It was the first time I was reading him directly, not as presented by the Sangh. I was dumbstruck. The first book I read, *Riddles in Hinduism*, blew my mind. After that I found everything I could that Babasaheb had written. I learnt about the many bitter circumstances that arose in his life, with which he had to deal. *Annihilation of Caste* gave me a clear understanding of how Brahminism was responsible for the establishment of the hateful system of caste hierarchy and discrimination. I came to recognise the true nature of the

RSS. How, through their claim of samrasata or harmony, they were subverting the possibility of equality, justice and social transformation. And what the politics was behind naming Dalits as neglected (vanchit) and Adivasis as forest dwellers (vanvasi), denying us our own identity.

I was now horrified by the song we sang routinely in the shakha—*manushya tu bada mahan hai/ tu Manu ki santan hai* (Man, greatness is your destiny/ You are Manu's progeny). The song celebrated humans as the offspring of Manu—the very Manu who had enforced the system of caste hierarchy in the well-known *Manusmriti*, who considered Shudras, women and avarna untouchables as less than animals. Such a person was being celebrated as a great sage and the ancestor of all humans? What could be more evil?

The closed doors of my mind had started opening up. I read the *Manusmriti* and realised that Babasaheb was right. The treatise should be burnt as Babasaheb had done in 1927 in Mahad. As I read more and more of Babasaheb, the more my rebellious thoughts took firmer shape. Ambedkar's writings sowed the seed of progressive thinking in me. A Dalit perspective helped me understand my personal, individual struggle against the Sangh as a collective struggle for identity, social justice and dignity.

Then I read Kabir, Periyar and Phule. I was no longer just a rebel. My desire for revenge was slowly becoming a desire for transformation. In place of the poetry I had written for my own pleasure and for the entertainment of others, suddenly emerged poems that raised burning questions. I burnt my old romantic poems, full of metaphors about beautiful dusky locks of hair and deep intoxicating eyes.

Now the mood of my poetry was rebellious. I wrote:

> Burning just the Manusmriti,
> Why did you stop at that, Babasaheb?
> Why didn't you burn
> All those volumes in which Manu resides,
> In the minds of the so-called uppers....

And about Ekalavya's devotion to his teacher:

> Why Ekalavya, did you sacrifice
> As a gift to your teacher, your thumb?
> Why didn't you cut off
> Dronacharya's head,
> So that no other Ekalavya
> Should be asked to give up his thumb
> By another Drona,
> And never would be born
> Ever again, those who follow Drona....

On Ram and Sabari:

> Raja Ramachandra,
> You did not leave
> With that Adivasi woman Sabari
> Even a half-eaten fruit,
> And you too kept faith
> With enmity against us.

Those days I wrote dozens of verses like this. The tone of my prose writing changed too, turned revolutionary. In place of abstract supposedly literary stories, emerged sharp, rough, troubling stories about Dalit life and oppression and struggle. I continued to read extensively. Periyar's *Sacchi Ramayan* (translated into Hindi from Tamil and once banned in Hindi; in English, translated as *The Ramayana. A True Reading*); Phule's *Gulamgiri (Slavery)*; L.R. Balley's *Hinduism: Dharm ya Kalank* (Religion or Stain), and *Sarita–Mukta* magazine reprints that took a strong stand against religious obscurantism and political authoritarianism. I read Babasaheb of course, and books about him, but also Osho, J. Krishnamurti, Ram Manohar Lohia, Jayaprakash Narayan, Madhu Limaye, Kishan Patnaik, Marx, Engels, Freud, Nietzsche. I read a number of contemporary Hindi writers too. All of these built my intellectual framework. I also read a lot of literature critical of the RSS. It wouldn't be too much to say that Ambedkarite and humanist thought liberated me from mental slavery. Egalitarian thought changed the direction of my life.

30

The so-called confidential letter of the Sangh

In 1996 I received a xerox copy of a supposedly confidential letter of the Sangh circulated by a Dalit organisation, BAMCEF—the All India Backward (SC, ST, and OBC) and Minority Communities Employees Federation—founded by Kanshi Ram. Reading it, the origins of the organisation became clear. The Brahminical, casteist, Manuvaadi social structure had kept us Dalits and Shudras in slavery for thousands of years. When this system started to crumble under modern education and the British rule, the utterly casteist Marathi Chitpavan Brahmins, led by Keshav Baliram Hedgewar set up the RSS in 1925. Its function was to use the façade of Hindutva cleverly, to protect and promote the old and rotten caste system and varna vyavastha (the four-fold social hierarchy promulgated by the *Rig Veda*). Women, Dalits and Backward Castes were to be eternal slaves. Systematically using nation, religion, culture, and nationalism as popular slogans to mislead the masses, they put us mentally in thrall to them, and we became blind followers. This is why Shudras or Backward Castes still carry the dead ideas of Brahminism on their shoulders, like proud pall bearers.

I began to understand another aspect of the writings of the thinkers of the Sangh. While I was in the Sangh, I had thoroughly read the writings of the second sarsanghchalak Madhav Sadashiv Golwalkar, known as Guru-ji Golwalkar. His famous book *Vichar Navneet* (*Bunch of Thoughts*) had characterised caste as a unique feature of the Indian social system, and had firmly supported it. What was for us Dalits a painful foundation of our lives was for the Sangh thinkers unique, special, something to be proud of.

The confidential letter of the Sangh that I read was addressed to the upper castes, exhorting them to make the caste system of Hindu society even stronger. It was only because of this caste system, the letter said, that Hindu society had survived. If not for the caste system, everyone would have become Muslim or Christian. In the name of samrasata or harmony, the letter encouraged the upper castes to bring educated, professional Dalits, Adivasis and Backward Castes together under Hindutva. They were advised to include us so that we can then be held in an inferior position. The letter also exposed the anti-reservation ideology of the RSS.

This letter was eye-opening. I became ever more convinced that religiously doctrinaire and fundamentalist organisations can never work for the welfare of Dalits. I felt that I was fortunate to have escaped that dark well—perhaps by fluke, but I had escaped. Thousands of Dalit youth like me were still roaming around in khaki shorts and white shirts and black caps, brandishing lathis and considering themselves blessed to be born as Hindus. Who was to rescue them from this dark well? These people call themselves proud Hindus, feel extreme contentment in this identity, while savarna Hindus, far from accepting them as equals, do not even consider them human.

One of my journalist friends, Surendra Prabhat Khurdiya, used to bring out a journal called *Sanyukt Ekta* (Collective Unity) from Shahpura, Bhilwara. He was courageous enough to publish this confidential letter of the RSS. The Sangh went after him. He was harassed viciously. Cases were lodged against him. Eventually, he was arrested, sent to jail. He got bail with great difficulty, but came out undeterred, even more aggressive. With even greater energy he continued exposing the hypocrisy of the Sangh and its anti-Dalit, anti-Adivasi agenda.

Comrade Khurdiya was so filled with rage and desire for vengeance that he spread mud mixed with minute shards of glass at many places where shakhas were held. He believed in confronting them head on. He wanted us to take them on in physical combat. But I believed in non-violence and legal modes of confrontation. Despite these contradictions, we remained friends for a long time. Then he suddenly disappeared, and after many years I learnt that he was in Delhi, working for the Dera Sacha Sauda, a religious organisation led by a spiritual head. He wrote a blog and was also writing regularly in national newspapers. Although he shifted towards a spiritual and motivational path, in his writings there was no glimpse of communalism.

One cannot tell in what direction he would have gone,

because as the RSS gains control of institutions and power, many intellectuals are changing their tune.

While I was working on my memoir, I came to know that Comrade Khurdiya passed away on 15 August 2017.

31

From Sanghi to rebel

To begin with, my motivation was personal vengeance; in time it grew beyond that. It's true that my battle initially was against the casteist Sanghis of the Maandal tehsil of Bhilwara district and their discriminatory practices, not against the RSS as a whole. But when my appeals even to the senior-most Sangh leaders went unheard, my anger grew and turned against the organisation itself. I had, of course, always had minor disagreements, always had questions to ask, an attitude that was not appreciated in the Sangh; but the casteist behaviour of the Sanghis of Maandal catalysed the sparks created by each separate point of resentment into an explosion.

Somehow I had full faith that the moment my complaint reached the higher echelons of the Sangh, the lower-level figures responsible for the outrage would be sharply admonished, perhaps even removed from the RSS. If not that, they would at the very least face severe censure. When absolutely nothing was done, when my complaint did not even receive an acknowledgement, I realised that there was an unbridgeable gap between word and deed. The full extent of the hypocrisy of the Sangh became painfully obvious.

There is no procedure in the Sangh for conveying the opinions and complaints of lower levels to the higher ups. Orders are conveyed from top to bottom, but for anything to go upwards from below is impossible. Every pracharak, every official, every senior swayamsevak in a responsible position, made sure to preface every utterance with—the most revered sarsanghchalak has said so. The authority of the sarsanghchalak was invoked whether relevant to the context or not. They could silence any voice by citing this authority. Earlier, the highly Sanskritised and stiff Hindi used by Sangh officials had awed me. My youthful mind found it convincing and forceful. But with the discrimination I faced, Sanskritised Hindi lost its hold over me. I found the courage to contest its regime of terror.

As it was, my constant questioning made Sangh officials uneasy, and they did not consider me to be a proper swayamsevak. Now that I had raised the issue of caste discrimination, things became worse. I became a headache to them, and they started avoiding me. Once I realised that no conversation with them was possible, I turned towards fresh audiences. I started targeting Dalit swayamsevaks. I was astonished to find that each Dalit to whom I spoke reported similar disheartening experiences in the Sangh, relating to his caste identity. For the first time I saw that this was not my personal pain, but that of every swayamsevak of my community. The difference was that they were willing to accept it quietly, and I was not.

These faithful swayamsevaks of the Sangh sympathised

with me, told me their own depressing stories, but each one also advised me to stop talking about my experience everywhere. The Sangh is a massive organisation, they said, you cannot challenge it head on, you must learn to work within it and move forward together. I realised that these Dalit swayamsevaks lacked courage, each one was in the Sangh at the behest or orders of some so-called upper caste patron, and it was futile to expect them to support me, still less my rebellion.

The battle was for my community, but it looked like I had to fight it alone. I wrote, and spoke, and contacted people, and published, and kept my story in circulation, and although nothing came of my efforts, at least I felt I was fighting. In response I received advice, and often animosity and admonitions, but it was clear to me that my struggle would continue and that I would never return to the RSS. My battle grew stronger. How strange that the Sangh had no answers to the questions of a Dalit swayamsevak like me, while other Dalit swayamsevaks had no questions to ask of the Sangh.

I found a pattern in the internal organisation of the Sangh, a connection between the representation of castes, the caste of office bearers and the leaders of the Sangh, and their relationship to the balance of castes in our society. This was my caste audit of the Sangh. I realised that Dalits and Adivasis were mere tokens. The real owners of the Sangh were Brahmins and Baniyas; there were a handful of Rajputs, but the control of the Sangh was in the hands of the former group. It was clear there would never be any place for us, our dignity and our self-respect were immaterial to them. They only want to use us to attack the Muslims, otherwise we did not matter at all. A more informed understanding of the caste politics of the Sangh gave a foundation to my feeling of rebelliousness.

It was not yet clear what my destination was, but the course of my journey was becoming clearer.

32

The Sangh and I confront each other again

All this while, though I had been working for Dalit–Bahujan politics and ideology in different ways, the fight against communalism was never out of my sight. In 1999, an Australian missionary Graham Staines, along with his two small sons, was burnt alive in Odisha by Dara Singh, a Sangh-inspired murderer of the Bajrang Dal. My friend Allaudin 'Bedil', who worked for the mill workers' union, and I launched a signature campaign in Bhilwara against this heinous act and publicised it. The local press was not fond of our militant language, but we continued to keep our campaigns sharp and uncompromising. Writing everywhere, going from village to village exposing the Sangh and its affiliates, and organising Dalit and Adivasi youth, these were my main activities at the time.

The lower levels of the Sangh often descended to even lower levels of behaviour. Coming face to face with them in villages, there were arguments and often physical confrontations. There would be blustering threats to break our limbs, but I didn't give a damn. If my limbs were to be broken, so be it. It could happen at the hands of Hindutvavaadi goons, or it could happen in an accident; and if it was not to be then it simply would not—nobody could harm a hair of my head. As for death, I was always prepared for that too. It was never my ambition to die coughing feebly in a hospital. Death is the final truth of life. Whenever it has to come, it will come, and I will welcome it. Every day I live with this knowledge, and this conviction gives me courage. I had no fear when I started my fight against the Sanghi forces all by myself, and I have no fear now that thousands of companions fight alongside me. I have always wanted to fight them on the ground, and that is what I continue to do, continuously exposing their poisonous ideology and violent activities.

Later, when I joined a government school as a primary teacher, the battle became sharper because the RSS had full control over Hindi medium primary school teachers.

When I was called to Maandal for teacher training, I took the decision to calm down a little, do my work, avoid politics and focus on my responsibilities as a teacher. I reached the thirty-day training programme with this intention. It was June 1999. But the moment I reached there, I had my first run-in, even before the first prayer meeting. Participants in the training programme were being welcomed with a tilak. This is a traditional practice of welcome in Rajasthan, tying a turban and applying a tilak—a vertical stripe of vermilion on the forehead. But I had a strong principled objection to this tilak. Do what you want at home, but why this kind of thing in a public institution? I raised an objection to welcoming government schoolteachers with a tilak. Some Muslim and Dalit participants supported me. We refused to allow them to apply tilak on our foreheads. The resource persons at the event were mystified: who are these crude illiterates who have entered the temple to Saraswati?

The next issue of contention was the prayer to the Hindu goddess Saraswati—'O player of the veena, give us your blessings'. I said we should sing another prayer, one which invoked different names of god, better reflecting all the different communities gathered there—'You are Ram, and you are Rahim, O merciful one; you are Krishna, Khuda, you are Wahe Guru, you are Jesus Christ; in every name you are present.' What blessings could the player of the veena give us? What work has she written, what verse has she given us? This goddess of education was perhaps herself illiterate. What could she possibly offer us?

At my saying this, there was uproar. The organiser of the training programme showed his displeasure, all the more so when I objected to the next song even more strongly. This was

> *Chandan hai is desh ki maati, tapobhoomi har gram hai/*
> *har bala devi ki pratima, baccha baccha Ram hai.*
> Fragrant as sandalwood is the earth of this land, every village a pilgrimage/ Every girl the image of the goddess, every child is Ram.

I said this is not a shakha that you can force us to sing an RSS song here. We are here to be trained as teachers and it would be best for you to stick to the songs listed in the training material and module, or else I will be forced to lodge a complaint. The result of this strong objection was that all of it disappeared—

the Hindu prayers and rituals and tilaks. Songs and prayers were now all-faith.

But I was now in their sights. My documents were examined, enquiries were launched about this insufferable boy who was breaking the discipline of the training camp.

After lengthy consultations between the organiser of the training and the resource persons, I was summoned—'Have you come here to become a leader and do politics, or to be trained as a teacher? This will not be tolerated.'

I introduced myself and said firmly that you can send me home, but I will not permit this training to be run like a shakha of the RSS. I will lodge formal complaints against all of you, and also take the matter to the press. The resource persons got scared. We arrived at a compromise. There would be no RSS propaganda, and I would not stir up further trouble.

But this incident brought me into politics here too. Over two academic sessions, I worked to organise and lead the teachers of primary schools. We were ninety-nine in one batch, and through them I reached almost every village in Maandal tehsil. In January 2001, seven of us launched a monthly called *Diamond India*, which was meant to attack communalism, casteism and corruption. It was well received as a secular initiative to make India into a valuable and pure diamond.

But such praise does not last long. As *Diamond India* started to expose the truth about many things, casteist, communal and corrupt forces joined together against us. The Sangh backed them, and all those in the Sangh who had been angry with me for years took the opportunity to attack me frontally. Thus the Sangh and I came face to face once again.

33

My family and my experience as a teacher

We completed our training and I went to my allotted school, the primary school at Dhannaji ka Kheda, two kilometres from Sirdiyas, and part of Sirdiyas panchayat. This was a village of Gurjars, a Backward Caste community whose work was agriculture and animal husbandry, and who observed untouchability with utmost stringency. I was skeptical of my ability to teach in such a place, expecting some sort of confrontation here too. The future seemed uncertain. Unsurprisingly, my experience as a teacher here was most dispiriting.

The tragedy of the Backward Castes is that they consider themselves pure Hindus and, under the sway of Hindutva, are at the forefront of committing atrocities against Dalits. But they have no sense of their own position. They are like the peacock that dances in a trance, filled with admiration for itself, never looking down at its ugly feet, for were that ugliness revealed, it would be impossible to maintain the illusion of its own perfect beauty. If we ask these foot soldiers of Hindutva what their own position is in the caste hierarchy of Sanatana Hinduism, they are stumped. When forced to accept that they are Shudras, their faces darken. The truth is so bitter it is impossible for them to accept. Pushed to the wall by its force, they start blustering, loudly repeating the hollow formula, 'Say it with pride, we are Hindus!' The Manu whose law made them lowly Shudras, they honour; and the Babasaheb whose Constitution made them humans, they look upon with hatred, treating him as a hero for Dalits alone, distancing themselves from him.

This is the distinguishing feature of Backward Castes today—considering themselves superior and proving this by attacking and humiliating Dalits. These Shudras fail to understand that the other three 'upper' castes watch these activities with amusement and joy. It's fine by them if the lower castes and outcastes are at each other's throats, so that they never get together to turn their attention towards the real oppressors.

The Backward Castes don't consider Kabir, Phule or Ambedkar to be theirs. Nor do they consider Gandhi, Ram Manohar Lohia, Jayaprakash Narayan or Vishwanath Pratap Singh to be their own. It is the RSS they feel close to, and its equality-hating thinkers are the ones they appreciate. What can be done about such fools? In every shakha today, morning and evening, the most active in their khaki shorts, jumping around busily, are the Shudras, ever ready to take lives and give their own lives for Hindutva. Not that the Sangh has any place for them in its leadership structure. Still, large numbers of the youth of Backward Castes roam around clutching to themselves the practically dead body of Hindutva.

So it was in this village of such Backward Castes, Dhannaji ka Kheda, that I was to embark upon imparting 'joyful learning'. How was I to do this with children who looked upon me with disgust? The children I was to teach had been already indoctrinated with the idea that the new teacher was of a lower caste. You are not to drink water touched by his hand, not even accept dry grain at lunch-time from him.

Already, before the session started, the villagers had come to me and insisted that there be separate containers of water for their children and me. I flatly refused this demand and told them they could follow these practices of untouchability in their own homes, not in a government school. Here, all are equal, I said. They didn't argue much, but from the next day the children started getting bottles of water from home, or they drank from the well in the school compound. They just would not drink water from the same container I used. I thought, to hell with it. Let them drink or die of thirst, why should I care. In that entire village there was not a single family or individual with whom I could sit and chat for a while, or whose home I could enter.

These people could not bear to even see me ride my cycle past their homes. They would accost me: 'Mastersahab, at least in the village, get off your cycle'. Finally I stopped going to the village altogether and stopped inviting the villagers to school on national festivals. An undeclared state of tension and non-communication existed between me and the villagers. Somehow, I continued to teach but there was no joy in it. I wanted to run away, somewhere far where my caste would stop following me.

Even now, in primary and high schools, the caste discrimination prevalent in the education sector affects not only Dalit students, but Dalit teachers too, routinely forcing them to face insult and bitter humiliation. I realised during my two years of teaching that in many villages my Dalit colleagues could not even sit on chairs to teach. At places, if the school's mid-day meal was touched by a Dalit teacher or student, the entire food would be thrown away. Unable to bear this kind of humiliation, Mohanlal Regar, a teacher and a resident of Anjana, committed suicide. The discrimination against Dalits continues in schools till today. But the centuries-old habit of accepting this injustice is equally prevalent among Dalits themselves.

Since childhood, I had imbibed from my father certain values that ran in his family, a culture of resisting injustice.

My father, Narayan Lal Meghwanshi, is a farmer, keeps livestock, and is also a village-level leader. His family and my mother Dhanni Bai are from the weaver caste of Bunkar, which makes its livelihood from farming, keeping livestock and weaving. It is said that some two hundred and fifty years ago, my father's ancestors settled in Sirdiyas village, having left Antali village of Asind taluka in Bhilwara district. However, faced with unending caste discrimination, my ancestors set up a separate village called Balaikheda, to all intents and purposes a part of Sirdiyas village, but at a distance from it. Originally my ancestors were from the deserts of western Rajasthan, where they were called Meghwal.

According to the census of 2011, Sirdiyas has a total of 310 houses, with a population of 1,660 (847 men and 813 women). Of these, 232 are Dalits and ninety-five Bhil Adivasis. Like in other villages of India, untouchability is woven into the very fabric and structure of Sirdiyas village. Sirdiyas was dominated by Gujjars who comprised sixty per cent of the population, and there were also a handful of Jats, Maalis (gardeners), Rajputs, Naayis (barbers), Yogis (Nathpanthi), and Vaishnavs—there were no Brahmins.

My mother Dhanni Bai is eight years younger than my father. They were married as children, but she started living in my father's home later, at the age of fifteeen, as is a common practice in Rajasthan. She is a woman of untiring energy and an efficient manager of the household, from livestock to farming, as of the home itself. Had she been educated, she would have been a notable administrator. She has magic in her fingers, and can smooth away stomach-ache and back-ache with her expert massages. She is very gentle and kind, she tells me that I used to cling to her as a child, and insisted on feeding at her breast till the age of five. If I fell ill she would be frantic with worry. Once when I was bitten by a snake, and had to be taken by cycle to the nearest hospital seven kilometres away, she ran alongside the cycle and reached the hospital practically at the same time. I have always been very close to my mother. She taught me right from wrong in the most loving manner. I hated taking baths, cried and wailed, but she used to patiently coax me into bathing. I also used to make a huge fuss about drinking milk, sometimes knocking the glass over, and got a couple of slaps for it too, but her love for me was always clear. When my elder brother and I went to Ayodhya on karseva, she wept and wept, and didn't eat properly till we returned. She couldn't say 'Ayodhya', pronounced it 'Ayujya', but how she cursed the RSS!

Even writing about her makes me emotional—towards her I still feel like a small child.

I learnt compassion from my mother, and fearlessness from my father.

Father had taught us never to come home having been beaten up by anybody. If somebody slaps you once, turn around and slap him twice. If he is stronger than you, hit him and quickly run away, but never come back home with your tail between your legs. My father was one of six brothers and three sisters, each one a solid fighter who never took an injustice lying down. They would tell us stories about how they fought against the so-called upper castes. Long years ago, as a result of such fights, they had left the village and come to live in their fields, where nobody could control them.

One time, when our fields were being irrigated by canals running from the pond, the thakur of the village, the local landlord, tried to stop our water supply and abused my father's brother, my tau. That was it. My father and all his brothers and sisters landed up at the canal and, at a time when feudalism was at its height, they beat the hell out of the thakur. The entire village watched their arrogant thakur being dragged and beaten all the way back to his own doorstep. From that day on, the villagers learnt their lesson. Nobody dared to raise a hand against our people after that.

From childhood I had heard such heroic stories from my father.

In this matter my father is my idol. Even today he believes in responding to violence with equal force, and always keeps his licensed gun loaded. At his age—seventy-six now—he is still cool and fearless. I don't think I have his courage. Nevertheless, if I am not a coward, it is thanks to him. He taught me to stay away from fear, and to understand that if one loses one's life fighting injustice, it's worth it, one should never live in fear and never put up with injustice.

My father was elected sarpanch (head) of Sirdiyas from 1995 to 2000, under the provisions of the 72nd and 73rd Amendments to the Constitution, which established reservations in local bodies. He was the first elected Dalit sarpanch of our village. The local thakur, Shiv Singh, had fielded his domestic help as the rival candidate. Their campaign against my father was that despite being a nobody, he still struts about like a leader, sits on the same level as others, fears nobody, listens to nobody. Imagine his arrogance if he becomes sarpanch! But despite all this, he gathered the votes of the OBCs of Haripura village, which was part of Sirdiyas panchayat, and managed to win.

In 1999, the Ashok Gehlot-helmed Congress government decided to open Rajiv Gandhi Swarna Jayanti Pathshalas (named to commemorate the late prime minister's golden jubilee) in villages and localities having a population of more than two hundred but with no facility for elementary education. Some eighteen thousand schools sprang up, including in Dhannaji ka Kheda and Sajjanpura villages that came under our panchayat's jurisdiction. The power to appoint teachers to these schools was vested with the gram sabha, village council, headed by the sarpanch. My father being the sarpanch, I was appointed as a teacher in one such school.

I have already described how nasty the upper caste villagers were towards me, but worse was still to come. One day I reached school a little late. In the meanwhile, two students had got into a fight and were injured, one of them was bleeding. The guardians of the child arrived at school to fight with me. I could understand that they would want to question me and complain to me, but they surpassed all limits, shouting casteist abuse at me at the top of their voices. I bore it quietly for a while, but when it continued, I started shouting back and advanced on them with a stick. They retreated at this, but did not stop their invective and their terrible curses at my capabilities and my caste. The indignity gnawed at me. I could not endure it.

I stopped going to school for many days, thinking what's the point, I teach high ideals but am unable to live up to them, why should I continue to be a teacher. Ultimately I went to the higher officials and tendered my resignation, freeing myself altogether from the mayajaal, from all illusion.

34

Meeting with a Sufi dervish

It seemed I just kept absconding from every place, filled with restlessness. I was quite sick of all religion, but there was a kind of spirituality in me that urged me towards the unknown. At home I had heard Kabir's nirgun bhajans, his songs in praise of the formless. My grandparents had been quite involved with prayer meetings and enjoyed being in the presence of sadhu–sants, sages and ascetics. There were often Dalit sages who visited our home. They sang the songs of Bhakti saints like Kabir and Ravidas and of saints from the Dalit Meghwal community like Rupade and Dharumegh, and of Likhmoji of the Maali community, all believers in nirgun bhakti, faith in the divine as formless. My father too would sing beautiful bhajans on the veena. They would travel far to attend prayer meetings, and as singers of bhajans they had a fine reputation.

My mother did not sing bhajans along with the men, but as was the practice in our area, while the men sang, she would join the women who gathered at a little distance to sing spiritual songs. Bhajan was what men sang, spiritual songs—adhyatmik geet—was the name given to what the women sang. Women did sit with the men in satsang, during prayer meetings, and they sang bhajans too. But my mother never did. She knows countless Rajasthani songs by heart, which she sings on different occasions.

Ever since I grew conscious of the world, this had been the atmosphere at home, spiritual, religious. My father would also conduct the puja at the temple to our family deity, Ramdev-ji, in our village, and I inherited this legacy from the age of eight, going to do puja there in the morning and evening. People even called me pandit, the honorific given to a Brahmin priest. I learnt in childhood to read the panchang, the Hindu calendar. From the age of twelve, I could calculate auspicious times for specific events, read omens, tell people their future based on the movements of stars and planets.

After I joined the RSS, I studied Sanskrit seriously. In class eleven, I had studied Geography, but in class twelve I studied Sanskrit instead. I learnt shlokas, started the study of Vedic texts, and aspired to be a master scholar. I also studied samudrika shastra, the science of face reading, and got interested in palmistry, reading the famous palmist Cheiro. Now I would read people's palms, and interpret their horoscopes based on the time of their birth.

My family deity was a pir, a saint called Ramdev of Runija, believed to be a Raja and also the twenty-fourth avatar of Vishnu. At Ramdevra in Jaisalmer, in Pokharan block, is a temple dedicated to him, where every year more than three million people arrive in pilgrimage. Now people of all faiths accept him as their god, and walk all the way to Ramdevra. But till about twenty years ago, Ramdev Pir was the deity of Dalits alone. Even today in Rajasthan, Gujarat and Malwa you will find a Ramdev temple in every Dalit settlement.

In my village, the temple was built some sixty years ago, and conducting puja in it was my family's responsibility. Till today we are the pujaris, priests, of the Ramdev temple. For about a decade I conducted the puja and worship of Ramdev. I was part of bhajans, prayer meetings and gatherings of sadhu–sants, but I never really experienced Ramdev-ji in my heart, nor did I learn the bhajans or how to play the dholak–manjira, the instruments that accompanied bhajan singing. Not one bhajan could I learn by heart. The outward performances of religion were all around me but I felt nothing inside.

My father was a bhajan singer, a member of the panchayat and also a tantrik, practising occult arts. He knew how to extract the poison of snakes and scorpions with mantras, how to control evil spirits, make amulets, perform exorcisms, rouse cremation grounds and other such tantrik skills. People know him as Janter or Tantrik and would often take him with them to perform these arts. Once I said to him, teach me the mantras, I want to learn these skills too. He told me, 'Son, these are all fake. Let these tricks remain with me. There are no ghosts, no witches; spirits do not arise from cremation grounds, nor do any mantras work. This is all just popeleela—illusions and trickery. Don't ever get into this.'

He never did let me do it. He didn't like me to read palms, horoscopes and the panchang either. All rubbish, he said.

He does not believe in any god other than Ramdev-ji, but his devotion towards him also bound me. I too had to go to the temple and do puja, my father would not tolerate any carelessness there. In the beginning I did not know much about Ramdev-ji, only that he was our family deity. I decided as a child to learn all about him, and much later, after two years of serious research, I wrote a paper, "Ramdev Pir: A Re-examination", which was published as a book in 2006.

Through this research I came to know the truth about Ramdev Pir, whom the RSS had appropriated, calling him the Sun of Hinduism, claiming that he died fighting against marauding Mughals while protecting cows. This turned out to be completely false.

Moreoever, the legends around Ramdev Pir are very complicated. Folk belief is that he was born into the family of a Dalit saint, Sayar Jaypal, and was then inducted into the tutelage of Guru Ajmal Tanwar. He is said to have been influenced by Sufis of the Muslim Ismaili Nizari sect, and taken deeksha, religious initiation, from them. He then roamed the desert regions preaching the true religion, promoting the uplift of Dalits. Six hundred years ago, he gave women equal status in the community prayer meetings. Because of this he was accused of being a proponent of free sex, and was declared a 'kanchaliyapanthi'. This derogatory term comes from the calumny that the followers of this sect practised sex as worship. It is believed that its members, husbands and wives, went for worship after 11 pm, where, after bhajans and puja, the women's bodices were placed in a pot (kanchali is the word in Rajasthani for bodice or breastcloth). The men were blindfolded, and whichever woman's bodice they picked from the pot, they had sex with her. Semen is the prasad and this sexual intercourse was believed by the sect to be sacred and to bring about moksha, or liberation from the cycle of reincarnation.

I have never actually come across an instance of such a form of worship, nor has anybody to my knowledge. I believe that sects like the Satpanth or Sirate Mustaqeem of Ramdev Pir are mocked as kanchaliyapanthi simply because they permit men and women to sit together in satsang and give them equal respect.

Ramdev Pir faced so much harassment that he took samadhi, voluntarily embracing death in a religious ritual, at the young age of thirty-three, in Runija. His sister and first disciple Dalibai had already taken samadhi two days earlier.

When I wrote about all this in my book, many people were angry with me, but soon they accepted that I was presenting the truth. Ramdev had dedicated his entire life to the transformation of the lives of untouchables, and so Dalit followers of the Alakhnami and Nirgun sects, both of whom meditate upon the formless, were drawn to him in large numbers. The publication of books by Ramprakashacharya, Dr Kusum Meghwal and myself also contributed to the recognition of Ramdev as a Bahujan leader in the growing movements of assertion among Dalit–Bahujan and Adivasi or Moolnivasi (indigenous) communities.

Spirituality was very much a part of my life from the beginning, but at the same time my tendency to use reason and rationality made me uncomfortable in most religious spaces. After giving up teaching, I was talking to my friend Allauddin 'Bedil' one day and I said, 'My mind is just not at peace; let's go to someone who has the spiritual power to comfort me.' My friend was a cool kind of guy, and he immediately said, 'In Ahmedabad there is a Sufi saint, Sailani Sarkar. Let's go to him.'

I remembered that in 1996, a Sufi saint of this name used to live in Bhilwara in the shanties of the nomadic Banjara people at Police Lines. He was attacked virulently in a newspaper owned by an RSS office-bearer, in the style of a sensational exposé, with the allegation that Sailani Sarkar, a Muslim godman, was an agent of the Pakistani secret service, ISI. It was also alleged that vehicles visited him at night, bearing arms and money, which was distributed in Bhilwara. The point of this scandalous story was to focus the attention of the police on Sailani Sarkar whenever there were incidents of communal violence in Bhilwara. It was further claimed that Muslims came to him from everywhere but he had no time for Hindus, whom he drove away with curses.

The story spread confusion among people. They began to wonder who this mysterious Sailani Sarkar was, and why he was staying among the Banjaras. Was he a tantrik or a fraud? Loyal to India or a Pakistani agent? There was uproar. The police and administration, supported by communal forces, brought in bulldozers and razed the settlement of the poverty-stricken Banjaras to the ground. But Sailani Sarkar could not be found. Bhairu Bhai Banjara and his wife Badam Bai Banjara were arrested for resisting the police action on their settlement. And of course nothing of what the newspaper story claimed—arms, ammunition, money—was found there.

At around this time, there was also talk about a lawyer called Munna Khan Pathan and his Ambassador car that had 'Sailani Sarkar' written on it. He informed the administration that Sailani Sarkar was a Sufi dervish, a saint, whose goal was to promote love and brotherhood, and to serve humanity, that he had no interest in worldly matters, and there was no foundation to any of the allegations against him. That all this was a conspiracy to remove the settlement of the Banjaras.

I was then the editor and publisher of a newspaper called *Dahakte Angaarey* [Smouldering Embers], which I brought out between 1992 and 1998—the year I got my teaching job.

Having been a keen reader of *Panchjanya* and *Osho Times*, I had long been interested in the idea of bringing out a periodical. While in the RSS I had started a handwritten newspaper called *Hindu Kesari* in 1991. It was of four pages and contained material about the Sangh's ideology. Starting *Dahakte Angaarey* was the next step in that journey, although the first issue was on Pakistan, since I was still under the influence of the Sangh. It did not come out regularly, just whenever funds could be organised.

As editor of *Dahakte Angaarey*, I tried to meet the Sufi saint and also the Banjaras, who were facing harassment from the Sangh affiliates. I could not meet the saint, but did manage to meet Bhairu Bhai Banjara and the lawyer Munna Khan Pathan.

On the basis of this I published a story titled "Sailani Sarkar: Sangh gang cooks up a baseless controversy". My interest arose from the fact that the RSS, the VHP and the Bajrang Dal were all after this one person—who *was* he? My story did play an important role in exposing the RSS for its lies, but by that time Sailani Sarkar had gone to Ahmedabad.

This was the Sailani Sarkar to whom Bedil Sahab took me on 20 August 2000. We met him in the locality of Danilimda, early in the morning. I just couldn't understand the whole situation. No dargah, no puja, no namaz. Nothing at all that could be seen as spiritual or religious. Just this ancient person. In ordinary clothes, white hair, physically frail, completely unlike anything I had imagined.

In my experience, sages and ascetics had been fairly well-fed specimens. Big paunches, dreadlocked hair, saffron robes, long beards, but this person displayed none of these. Not even a beard such as Muslims have, or a cap on his head. More ordinary than ordinary people. There was absolutely no way he looked like a saint to me. I was thoroughly disappointed, what a waste of time to have come so far.

He asked me, 'From where have you come, and why?' My friend Bedil said, 'To have a deedar—to see you with our eyes, to be in your presence.' The Sufi saint got very angry at this. 'Take deedar of me? Who am I? Am I god? The lover's portrait is in your own heart, just bow your head, and you get your deedar. Haven't you heard, *Where do you wander, my servant, searching for me, I am always close to you.*' It was a song by Kabir he invoked. 'Why do you stray here and there, your god is within you. Leave now, and never come back. Come to take deedar indeed!'

Turning us out, he said 'Everyone comes to ask something of god, nobody comes asking *for* god.'

Then he turned to me, put a hand on my shoulder, and said, 'All this anger is no good. Go now, and give the message of humanity and brotherhood to people of all castes and religions. Write books, and turn these stones of Hindustan into diamonds.'

I liked his style, bereft of ritual and hypocrisy, so simple and ordinary, so straightforward. I was instantly smitten by this Sufi dervish Sailani Sarkar, and later we became friends, a friendship that lasted till his death in 2018. A deep spiritual relationship. Neither did he think of giving me religious initiation, deeksha, nor did I ever think of becoming his disciple. It was a loving relationship of humanity and mutual caring. People would ask, what do you have that's so deep, the two of you? I would fall silent. Lines from Kabir's doha would come to mind:

> *Akatha kahani prem ki, kuch kahi na jaay/ Goonge keri sharkara, baithe muskaay.*
> Of the untold story of love, what can be said really/
> When the mute savours candy, he just smiles sweetly.

There was an exhilaration to it.

Our first meeting resulted in a monthly journal, *Diamond India*, with its goal of turning the stones of India into diamonds.

It ran for twelve years.

My interest in fostering humanity and brotherhood continues till today. I have no interest in organised religion, nor a need of it. Now temples and mosques and gurudwaras are all the same to me. God appears in humans, and standing with those in pain is what fulfils me.

Now, like Kabir, I feel

> *Bhala hua meri maala tooti, Ram bhajan se chhooti, mere sir se tali bala....*
>
> Good thing my prayer beads shattered; chanting Ram's name no longer matters; what a load off my head!

All puja and incense and all of that, is now in my mind alone. Kabir and the thoughts of Buddha have transformed my life. I need no god nor divinity. Whatever I am now, I'm fine.

35

The publication of *Diamond India*

After meeting the dervish Sailani Sarkar I decided to start a monthly journal—but funds? Who would contribute? Who would help? I discussed this with my colleagues in schoolteaching, and one day we landed up at the government-allotted residence of a friend of ours in the Maandal block panchayat, Lakshman Gurjar. Seven comrades assembled—Kan Singh Rathore, Girdhari Lal Gurjar, Balvir Singh Gaur, Paras Lohar, Bhairulal Sharma, Pappu Singh Chundawat, and myself. I announced my decision to give up employment and do journalism, and asked for their cooperation. I will remain grateful to these friends all my life. To whatever I am today, their contributions are unforgettable.

We formed a company under which we started *Diamond India*. Thirteen more friends joined in this endeavour, among whom were Harisingh Bhati, Mevaram Gurjar, and Manju Sharma. We decided that the journal would combat communalism, casteism and corruption, and spread the message of love, solidarity and humanity. We would not accept any advertisements, nor would we publish stories that promoted intoxicants, superstition or fantasy.

On 14 January 2001, the first copy of *Diamond India* was published. Initially people thought it was a trade magazine of diamond merchants. The title seemed entirely as if it was about business, but inside, the journal was fiercely opposed to commodification and market forces. Soon it became very popular. Our team wrote in the simple and everyday language that our readers liked. We published investigative reports, and offered a third view about polarised and contested incidents, which was welcomed by the people.

Our readers used to say that when they read *Diamond India,* it was like having a conversation. We distributed the journal far and wide, even to small and distant villages. Clashes with the organisations affiliated to the Sangh were common. In Rajasthan, the RSS mouthpiece *Pathey Kan* reaches every village, and through it the Sangh ideology and propaganda reach large numbers of people. Nobody had tried to counter them in this. *Diamond India* did. In villages where the Sangh was very influential, we garnered large numbers of readers. People were now getting to read two kinds of opinion, and our journal was beginning to be accepted as an alternative. We never hesitated to frontally attack communalism and casteism.

The demand for the journal was growing, and we were encouraged. We started with a hundred copies of the first issue, and went up gradually to five thousand copies a month. We used to send them to subscribers by post. We opened an audio division of *Diamond India*. Cassettes were very popular in those days, and people used to listen to them on tape recorders. Our first cassette was *Arise, Sons of Bharat*. This was a long speech against the RSS and other Hindu and Muslim extremist organisations, which I had delivered at a 'cadre camp' for Dalit and Adivasi youth. (Cadre camps are popular in Dalit–Bahujan circles where for one whole day classes are offered in anti-caste literature and thought.) It was a rousing and even inflammatory speech—I admit it. This is the training I had received in the Sangh, which has never left me. The cassette became quite controversial. At this time the Sangh was spreading its poison all over the country with cassettes of the hate-filled speeches of two sadhvis, female ascetics. Mine was seen as a response to them.

The funny thing was, often, at many a crossroads, while the firebrand sadhvis Rithambhara and Uma Bharati were shrieking through their cassettes, my voice could be heard yelling back from paan shops nearby. The relentless counterblast exhausted the Sangh and they withdrew their cassettes. When they stopped, my supporters stopped playing my cassette as well. In this way, we replied to Hindu extremists in their own language and style. Through the journal, we had already started the battle of the printed word.

My colleagues were not very interested in ideology and so on. They were happy enough with the public response. However, this happiness was short-lived. The networks of the Sangh are so far-reaching that one seldom gets a full sense of their spread till they reveal themselves. So far the Sangh had either ignored my activities or responded lightly, but this time there was a systematic and organised attack. They knew that the entire team of *Diamond India* was in government employment. I had given up my government job, but the others hadn't, and it was natural for them to be worried when the Sangh started threatening them one by one. They stood to lose their sole means of livelihood if they were judged to be politically active, and so we decided that while their financial contribution would continue, their names would be removed from the journal.

Now the entire responsibility for *Diamond India* fell upon my shoulders, although my colleagues helped when they could. Meanwhile, the Sangh affiliates had started their offensive on our journal in different places. They would threaten people against becoming our members, and in every possible way they tried to get us to shut down the journal. It was evident that times were going to get very difficult for *Diamond India*; the Sanghis were determined to kill our ideas. Their propaganda against us was so relentless that countering it consumed the greater part of our energy.

Having brought out the month's issue of *Diamond India*, I was sitting in the Bhilwara office and reading the newspaper *Rajasthan Patrika* when I saw a news item that in Rajsamand, in Janavad village panchayat, a public hearing had been organised by the Mazdoor Kisan Shakti Sangathan, an organisation of farmers and workers. The public hearing had established that lakhs of rupees had been embezzled from village development works. I was intrigued by this unusual strategy of a public hearing, and wanted to learn more. The news item said that the first "National Convention on the Right to Information" was to be held the next day, at the Subhash Garden in Beawar.

I decided to attend it.

36

Thieves are on a roll; will no one call them out?

On 6 April 2001, I went to Beawar in Ajmer district to report on the first National Convention on the Right to Information. I was pretty arrogant about being a journalist, expecting special seating for the media and so on. There was nothing of the sort. A large raised stage on which a lot of people were seated, some of whom I recognised as the former speaker of the Lok Sabha, Rabi Ray; the senior, well-known Hindi journalist, Prabhash Joshi; and the chief minister of Rajasthan at the time, Ashok Gehlot. As for the rest of the diverse people on stage, I had never seen them before. Below, an audience of thousands. Stalls all around, selling literature, books, food; the atmosphere was like a fair.

I went up to the team conducting the event and tried to talk to them. Three or four people seemed to be managing the stage, among them a young woman in a sari. I introduced myself to her, gave her a copy of *Diamond India* and requested that a press note be sent to me. This young woman seemed uninterested, she took the journal, muttered yes–no indifferently, and sent me on my way. I found this very strange. At first I thought she was Aruna Roy, and was disappointed by her callous behaviour. Later I learnt that the woman was Sowmya Kidambi. She had dismissed me peremptorily not because of arrogance but because she was overwhelmed by a thousand responsibilities that day. In later days we would often laugh about this first encounter of ours.

Participating in this convention was a new and interesting experience for me. I bought a large number of publications from there, met a lot of people and returned to Bhilwara. The cover story of our May issue was titled after a line from a spirited Marwari song that had been sung by the Mazdoor Kisan Shakti Sangathan at the meeting: *Chorivado ghanon hogyo re, koi to munde bolo*/Thieves are on a roll; will no one call them out? The song referred to thieving of all kinds, from the petty thief in the village to the mighty and corrupt seated in Delhi, and called upon the people to raise their voices. Uff. What a stunningly powerful rendition it was. Listening to it, I seemed to have travelled a whole aeon. The song's power, how it rolled sweetly in my mother tongue, captivated me for days. The bitter truth put out so openly and bravely, I was speechless with admiration.

The person who led the singing was introduced as Shankar Singh. He lived in a village close to Beawar called Lotiyana. I was mesmerised by this man's singing style and his voice. I decided I would meet him at leisure some day, although the details of how were not clear at the time. I only knew that the desire to meet him was overwhelming. At the meeting for the first time I heard Aruna Roy speak, and saw Nikhil Dey managing the proceedings; later he spoke too. I could not but be deeply impressed. These people were absolutely fearless, putting their views forward with resolute strength. When I returned, I wrote a story of twelve pages, and sent ten copies of it to Devdungri in Rajsamand district, the headquarters of the MKSS.

Soon after this, on May 11, we conducted a public hearing in Dariba village panchayat in my district Bhilwara, at the behest of our friend Ghisulal Vishnoi. I was a panel member at this event conducted under the banner of Janhit Sangharsh Samiti (Committee of Public Interest Struggles). I had no idea of how to conduct a public hearing, but we pulled it off anyway. That too, at night. The porch of Ghisulal Vishnoi's house was the stage. For three hours the proceedings went on, before an audience of about three hundred villagers. The financial irregularities and illegalities in the development works carried out by the sarpanch, Banshilal, were uncovered meticulously, one after another. Later, around 11 pm, having completed the hearing, when we were having dinner on the roof of Vishnoi's house, we heard a commotion downstairs. Supporters of the sarpanch had arrived and a brawl had broken out between them and those at the public hearing. Soon the attackers turned their attention to us, the outsiders who had arrived to create enmity between villagers who had, for so long, lived together in harmony. The police had to be summoned to save us and take us back to Bhilwara. This had been a risky adventure, but through it, the extent of corruption that had emerged was conveyed in detailed reports to the development officer of the block panchayat, Suvana, along with a demand for a full investigation. A copy of this report was also sent to MKSS.

When copies of *Diamond India* with the report on the National Convention on the Right to Information, and those of the report on the public hearing at Dariba village reached the MKSS headquarters at Devdungri, they were quite curious and excited. They wondered about this energetic voice in their area of work, launching such an uncompromising attack on communalism, casteism and corruption. The MKSS Central Committee decided that someone should go meet the people who brought out *Diamond India* and set up a working relationship that would be mutually beneficial. For our part, we too were keen to tie up with the MKSS. Our goals seemed identical. A discussion was coming, this was evident.

However, the meeting did not take place at the time. We got caught up in our work, they in theirs. It was an incident of communal violence soon after that brought us together again.

In Bhilwara district, at the Asind block headquarters, there is a temple of the Gurjar community, Sawaibhoj Mandir, with a four-hundred-year-old mosque, Qalandari Masjid, in its premises. Inflamed by the RSS, a mob of Gurjar youth razed this mosque to the ground. Asind was the next Ayodhya, it seemed.

37

Asind turned Ayodhya: Parallels to Babri

In a village near Asind, Govindpura, stands a famous temple to a deity of the Gurjars, Devnarayan, popular all over Rajasthan. According to legend, the Bagdawat Mahabharat was fought here, in which the ancestors of Devnarayan had battled long and hard. Here too, during a short stay, a Mughal emperor had built a mosque to perform his namaz, which was still standing there. The well-known Rajasthani writer Lakshmi Kumari Chundawat, in her important book on the Bagdawat Mahabharat, says, 'I was surprised by the presence of a mosque amidst the temple complex of Sawaibhoj Mandir.' In other words, the existence of the mosque was acknowledged by the writer of the landmark book on Sawaibhoj. The significance of this observation will emerge soon.

Qalandari Masjid was not a functioning mosque, and namaz had not been held for years, but there it stood. Gradually, as Hindutva politicised the Gurjar community, the mosque became a burning issue among the youth. They decided to destroy this already diminished place of worship and on 27 July 2001, they brought it down.

I had often visited the Sawaibhoj Mandir and seen this mosque. The moment I heard of its destruction I rushed to the spot. The mosque had been completely demolished, and its rubble had been pushed into a deep pit which was being filled with water. In its place, a statue of Hanuman, Bajrangbali, had been already established. I took a few pictures and came back to Bhilwara. When the news hit the media and the Muslims of Asind raised their voice in protest, the whole country became aware of what had happened. Droves of journalists from print and visual media started landing up in Asind. It became an international issue. I too used to go there every day. Asind had become Ayodhya and Qalandari Masjid, the equivalent of Babri Masjid. Here too, a masjid had become shaheed, martyred, just like in Ayodhya. As pressure from the media mounted, and the administration continued to be shortsighted, tension grew.

Bhilwara had a Gurjar majority which pretty much ruled the roost. So this incident was met with silence from most quarters, even the secular sections. Some for fear of losing votes from a majority community, some for fear of physical violence. Nobody wanted to risk any kind of confrontation. I knew this act of destruction did not have the backing of the whole Gurjar community, and that it was initiated and carried out by people linked to the Sangh. Whether anybody else spoke up or not, I decided to make my voice heard. But where, to whom? A team of human rights organisations soon arrived in Asind and went to meet the district collector at the dak bungalow. This was my chance.

I went there too. Looking through the window, I recognised some faces—these were the MKSS people. Later, on meeting them all, I learnt that it was a fact-finding team from the People's Union for Civil Liberties, come to investigate the demolition of the Qalandri Masjid. Among them were Neelabh Mishra, Kavita Srivastava, Nikhil Dey and Shankar Singh. Some local stringers from newspapers and TV channels also landed up there.

Having reached there almost immediately after the destruction, I could speak as an eyewitness. It was also imperative to contextualise the history of the structure. I explained to them all how for so many centuries this ancient mosque had stood undisturbed in the Sawaibhoj temple premises, and how it had now been razed to the ground, and a statue of Hanuman was placed where it stood.

The temple trust was flatly denying that there ever had been a mosque in the premises. I made available to the human rights team all documents and photographs that established the presence of the mosque. I told them that Lakshmi Kumari Chundawat's book was still sold in the temple grounds, and that it acknowledged the presence of the mosque. I also told them that the main person responsible for the vandalism of the Qalandari Masjid was very close to a leader of the Congress.

Sometimes caste awareness is so strong that people forget all other beliefs and ideology. Whatever party or political ideology anybody belonged to, as Gurjars they came together as one, prepared to sacrifice everything for their caste interest.

I didn't give a damn. I kept up my efforts to reveal the truth, and to raise my voice to the extent I could. It came to my attention that the extremists were now planning to prevent the annual festival, the urs at the Bariya Mazar, also located in the premises of the temple. I informed the fact-finding team of activists of this and expressed my fear that if a Muslim even accidentally strayed into the temple, his life would be in danger. Sawaibhoj had become a garrison of bloodthirsty goons who had landed up from all around.

Some police and mediapersons had already been beaten up. It was altogether an atmosphere of terror. I felt I was alone in fighting this. The consequences were clear, but who was bothered about consequences? As always, I was bolstered by the feeling—let's see what happens! And nothing happened. Of course, my unpopularity grew, and I was honoured with the certificate of being anti-Hindu.

It is said that until not so long ago the priests of Sawaibhoj temple were Dalit. But over the last decade, they had gradually been removed. Here too, in the largest of the temples, Dalit priests had been dismissed some decades ago. Now Dalits do not even go to worship there, even though the descendants of Dalit priests have royal documents from ancient times establishing their rights.

After the demolition of the mosque, it was decided to hold a traditional ashwamedha yagna to purify the premises. A real horse is not sacrificed any more, of course. An image of the horse in jaggery is fed to the sacrificial fire, or an image in silver is given as gift to Brahmins. Dalits were publicly insulted at this ceremony. Despite all efforts at persuasion, Dalits were not allowed to sit around the sacrificial fire. This prohibition was announced openly by the Brahmin priests conducting the yagna in the presence of a certain Khandeshwari Baba. I was not at all in favour of Dalits participating in the yagna, but for me it was also a test case to see if these people who claimed all Hindus were brothers would really permit Dalits to participate in Hindu rituals. Here were Dalits demanding to be allowed in, while all the Hindutvavaadi organisations opposed it openly, and the priests were even cursing us.

I decided to speak directly to the supposedly enlightened Khandeshwari Maharaj and set out for Asind.

So enlightened was this Khandeshwari Baba that his name was preceded by the honorifics Shri Shri 1008 and pujyapadi (with venerable feet). Known to have stood on his feet continuously for years, the Baba had taken an oath to never utter a word. His devotees addressed him respectfully as daata (the giver). He had successfully excluded Dalits from every yagna he conducted in the area, from Sawaibhoj to Danta Payra village in Banera tehsil. Along with my comrades I landed up to meet him, and we were told, look he won't speak, but meet him anyway. He will speak only in signs. My friend from Jagpura, Girdhari Meghwal and I, along with some other friends, decided to take the lead in this conversation. And indeed, Baba-ji said nothing. Only stared us down with fiery reddened eyes. His devotees informed us that if he wanted, he could reduce us to ashes at that very moment. I felt a strong desire to be turned to ashes. So I declared, either Dalits will participate in the yagna or we will be turned to ashes, there is no third alternative. Whether you throw us in the sacrificial fire, or use mantras, we Dalits will participate in the yagna, and if not, we are very happy to be turned to ashes.

How could the poor man turn us to ashes, daubed entirely in ashes himself! Well, the net upshot of this controversy was that news of it spread far and wide, and attendance at the yagna was very thin. In this way, the horse of the ashwamedha yagna of Kaliyuga was stopped midway. The so-called religious folk, hypocrites all, were cross as two sticks.

38

Obstructing yagnas

In 2009, at a yagna conducted in Khandeshwari Baba's presence at Danta Payra village, the same discrimination was again shown to Dalits. This gentleman had an ashram here, which was built with voluntary labour from Dalits. Wood for the yagna was taken from Dalits, who also contributed financially. But when it came to making sacrificial offerings at the 108 fire pits, not one Dalit couple was permitted to participate. The Dalits of the village approached the district administration with a complaint, to no avail. Then they came to me. I went there, and had barely reached than the administration and Baba-ji came to their senses. They felt that the anti-yagna forces have arrived, the entire event is in jeopardy; so they hastily set up a committee to arrive at a compromise. The committee met at the Banera subdivision office, that is to say, on government premises. I proposed that at eight of the 108 fire pits, Dalit couples be permitted to offer sacrifice. This was rejected straight away and a written alternative proposal was read aloud, that separate fire pits would be constructed for Dalits, and Dalits would not be allowed to eat with the rest of the devotees.

The reading out of this insulting proposal by an official of the administration, the patwari, in a government office, and in the presence of senior administrative officials, made me furious. I addressed the administration directly and asked if an event held on public land could openly discriminate like this. Now I was determined not to participate in the yagna but demanded that the provisions of the SC/ST Prevention of Atrocities Act be brought against the organisers. The situation worsened. The administration told the yagna committee to immediately wind up and leave, the yagna was cancelled. Later the committee grudgingly agreed to allow Dalits to participate, but by then Dalits were angry, and refused. We insisted that this yagna could not be held on public land.

Ultimately the yagna was held but on the private land of some person. The preparations made for the earlier yagna and the flag remained there for a while until the flag itself was worn down by the elements. The Baba went to the district collector's office and broke down in tears. His supporters were enraged. The district head of the Shiv Sena Commando Force, Govind Mundra, rang me up and made a veiled threat—'In ancient days rakshasas, demons, used to stop yagnas. Today, in Kaliyuga, it's people like you who obstruct holy work. Today because of you, for the first time ever, there were tears in daata's eyes.'

I listened to him patiently and said, 'You can call me a demon or whatever, it makes no difference to me. As for the tears in your daata's eyes, because of people like him, hundreds of thousands of my Dalit brothers and sisters have tears in their eyes. Whose tears should I take care of, and with whom should

I cry? I don't care for the tears of a daata or baba, I care more for the tears of my people. This yagna cannot take place on government land, hold it somewhere else, we don't care.'

Then I hung up.

After this came threats from a patron of the yagna committee and a well-known, influential BJP leader, that these anti-Hindus will be shot dead. I sent back the challenge: Our guns too have live bullets, not sawdust. Do you think we are sitting back waiting to be killed? We are ready too, pick a time and let's test our strength.

He must have thought we would be terrified at the very mention of bullets, but when he saw the possibility of a real pushback, he quietly retreated.

We did not allow the yagna to be held on public land.

Another yagna in the same series was held in Tiloli village by Baba Balaknath. There too, Dalits were made to do all the work, but were then told they could only come to eat afterwards, not participate in the yagna. About sixty per cent of the population of this village were Dalits—educated, independent, organised, and associated with Babasaheb Ambedkar's mission. They made the issue public and protested strongly. In order to examine the situation on the ground, and to show solidarity with Dalit struggles, I went there along with the lawyer and head of the Centre for Dalit Rights, P.L. Mimroth, and Gopal Das, retired Rajasthan adminstrative service officer, expert in revenue matters and a Valmiki himself.

We met the aggressive Baba. An utter fool.

He said, 'People of lower castes cannot sit at the yagna.

This is our faith and dharma. But if they still insist, they can do so after imbibing the panchagavya—the traditional mixture of cowdung, cow urine, milk, ghee and curd.'

That is, we had to be purified by eating cowdung and drinking cow urine before we would be allowed to participate in the yagna. We were enraged and declared it inhuman to expect any self-respecting and intelligent human to eat the excreta of an animal. Only people like you can do this, we said. We will not take it lying down.

We were surrounded by the supporters of the Baba, but we challenged them directly—'If this is how you treat Dalits, we will not permit this yagna to be held under any circumstances'.

Then we left.

The next day I went to Jaipur and met the chief minister at the time, Ashok Gehlot, and asked him directly, 'So now in your rule, Dalits will have to eat cowdung?' He and other senior officials present were astonished that this kind of discrimination and humiliation was visited upon Dalits, and assured me that justice would be done. Chief minister Gehlot took up the issue with great sympathy and understanding, and appointed an official to deal with it. Along with the sub-divisional official and district administration, he tried to settle the controversy, making it clear that Dalit participation was mandatory. By this time, despite pleadings from savarna Hindus, Dalits refused to participate in the yagna. Dalits made it clear that they would not tolerate discriminatory behaviour and would resist it with all their might.

The organisers were forced to declare it a private, family

yagna, not a public one. At the end of this yagna a procession was to set out with the sacred material of the puja in earthen pots, kalash, but because it was supposedly a family yagna, no women from the village took part in the procession. Ritually, it is the women who carry the kalash on their heads. Now the priests had to do this, and people started laughing at them—oh, look at the pandits, they're carrying the kalash on their own heads! Facing mockery, the pandits were forced to place the kalash on a tractor during their procession.

So this yagna too was a failure. Because of our intervention, five big yagnas and several small ones had been disrupted, for which we received many insults, while I received the title of rakshasa or demon. This new honour I received quietly, thinking to myself—how often our ancestors must have been called by this name. What's the big deal?

I have no belief in rituals like yagnas, nor do I think the situation of Dalits will be improved in the slightest by their participation in such things. However, if some Dalits wish to participate in such public events, it is their constitutional right, and I will fight shoulder to shoulder with them to achieve it, now and in the future.

As for these babas, I never gave a damn about them, nor did I fear their supposed spiritual powers. I have always raised questions about such babas and will continue to do so. Our country supports some unparalleled kinds of foolishness. Here's a guy who decides to hold a pair of tongs, or chimta. He begins to be called Chimta Baba. There's another who has not bathed in years, not even washed his face or mouth, lives with the filth of the whole world upon him, he gets the name of Aughad Baba, the Unkempt Baba. Yet another was a kind of colourful character, he was called Rangeeleyshah Baba; another was a known womaniser, and he was called Randishah Baba, randi being the crude, local term of abuse for a sex worker. Many babas have grown their hair in tangles or dreadlocks, others roam about naked. These Naga babas stage a spectacle during the Kumbh Mela, charging in their hundreds, completely naked, to the sacred confluence of rivers for their shahi snan, royal bath, before other pilgrims enter the waters. Where else in the world would you see this ridiculous nanga daud or naked dash to the river dignified?

There's the baba who has acquired the title of master of yoga, Yogiraj, purely on the basis of being able to work his breath in such a way as to swell his stomach. He has achieved the status of Rajrishi, the advisor sage to the king, and wanders the realm, making people drink the juice of bottle gourds, the humble lauki, by the litre, and amassing a fortune out of it. Then there's the sage who advises people to drink their own urine; and there's Asaram and Sons, who, in the course of doling out advice on strategies to conserve semen, somehow landed up in jail on grave charges of sexual assault and rape. There's a Nityanand who nitya, every day, takes pleasure, anand, in sex, and there's the one whose slogan is 'take out your money'. Someone's sect is the true one; another has built heaven in the land of khap panchayats, caste councils that protect their honour fiercely. There's one who roams the country making money in the name of the helpless cow, and there are others who make their living by selling talismans and performing exorcism rituals.

Our outlandish land, and its bizarre plight.

The whole country is packed with holy men and women of every faith—babas and pandits, mullahs and moulvis, granthis and raagis, munis and sadhvis, nuns, pastors, fathers, lamas and karmapas and bhikshus....

All day long under huge tents, they offer guidance on good behaviour, a veritable flood of advice from religious texts. And yet, there is no end in sight to rapes, degeneracy, casteism, injustice, oppression, corruption, lies, scams, murder. Our country, which pats itself on the back for its spiritual superiority, is the biggest hypocrite in the world. Animals are worshipped, cats and dogs are kept as beloved pets, they eat with their masters, but Dalits cannot even be touched. We are not even considered to be humans, but it is expected of us that we should prove our nationalism and praise our country as the best in the world, while sacrificing ourselves for the great Sanatana dharma of Hinduism. We should exchange our trousers for khaki shorts, and sing the RSS prayer, *namaste sada vatsale hindubhume,* day and night. Meekly take whatever is dished out to us and stay quiet. Is this possible? Absolutely not, never, not at any cost. Call us rakshasas or Hindu haters, or enemies of dharma, we don't care.

We will continue to raise the voices of our people, and speak out with all our strength. This resolve only grew in strength with time.

39

Equality before the law

My comrades and colleagues had some questions about my role in making public and criticising the demolition of the Qalandari Masjid. The special issue of *Diamond India* in September 2001 was on this topic and created a huge controversy. I was accused of taking money from Hindus and then writing against them. Some of my comrades found this argument convincing, so they pulled out their financial contribution and left the collective, but the majority remained with me. We then brought out a special issue against communalism, drawing attention to growing extremism in all religious communities, and attacking the trend. It was widely read and appreciated. But as our attack on casteism, communalism and corruption grew stronger, the slow choking of our resources by precisely those forces became more evident. We did not accept advertisements and managed solely on subscriptions. But now new subscriptions were becoming difficult, as the Sangh affiliates had announced that our journal was anti-Hindu. We made it to the end of our first year with great difficulty.

We had planned a poets' gathering at Manak Chowk to celebrate the first anniversary of the journal. As we began making the list of invitees, it occurred to us that we should invite the farmer-poet Shankar Singh who had written and sung *Chorivado ghanon hogyo re* at the National Convention on the Right to Information. Kansingh Rathore, Paras Lauhar and I went to Devdungri to meet him. The headquarters of MKSS was there, but when we reached, we found nothing as impressive as a 'headquarters', just a couple of tiny mud structures in which they lived. We asked about Shankar-ji, we were told he is coming soon, please wait. So we waited, the three of us. I felt rather silly. I had built up these people to my friends, but here was nothing that matched my praise. A former IAS officer Aruna Roy, the son of a senior air force officer Nikhil Dey, and the famous cultural activist Shankar Singh—did these people actually live here, in these mud huts? I was feeling really let down, wondering what my friends would be thinking. Where has he brought us, to these mud huts! How great he made them out to be, but no sign of greatness here.

And at this moment, a heart-wrenching scene unfolded. There, walking towards us, with rolls of cloth on their heads to support pots of water, were the farmer-poet Shankar Singh, and, behind him, Nikhil Dey. Who are these people, they are just like us, I had thought they would be very different. Special! But these were less than ordinary. Anyway, now that we were there, we decided to offer our invitation. If they accept it that's fine, and if not, that's even better. Once they had set down their pots, we told them about our programme and why we were there. They were thrilled to know that we publish *Diamond India*. We chatted. They invited us to stay for a meal, so lovingly that there was no question of saying no. Rotis made on the mud stove and a simple dal. We had to help ourselves. Here everyone did their own work, we were told. Later we washed up our own plates also.

Social activists are really strange. I had formed some impressions about them earlier, that they fly around in aeroplanes but wear rubber slippers. Speak in English, do not bathe for days. Wear all sorts of clothes. I never really understood them. The middle class ones among them spend their whole lives finding fault with their own class, but they really trust only those of their class, and help only them to move forward in life. That the social sector in India is two-faced and shifty. Like ostriches, they live with their heads buried in their own affairs. Nobody can match them in hypocrisy. Couldn't bear hunger themselves and have never known hunger, but deliver moving speeches about hunger. Conduct seminars on hunger in hotels where meals cost three thousand rupees a plate. Talk about change but do not change themselves one bit. They interfere in all sorts of things that don't concern them. Talk so much they don't get the time to act, these revolutionaries. These were some of the opinions I held about activists in the social sector, and of course, that those who held forth about social transformation were all Leftists.

Before I arrived in Devdungri, I did not even know there was a difference between a funded organisation or NGO (sanstha) and a non-funded political collective, a people's movement (sangathan).

But here everything was quite the opposite of what I had thought. These people had appeared so grand, but here they did the most menial things for themselves. I thought to myself, this mud hut is just for show, they actually live somewhere else, but why should we care, we just had to deliver the invitation to the poetry festival and go back.

On 26 January 2002, at the poetry festival organised in Maandal, the MKSS team arrived on time. They enacted a play called *Khajana* (Treasure) before reading poetry. They sang *Chorivado,* and stayed through the night. The audience was thrilled by them, much more than by the other poets who performed. Shankar Singh-ji had a puppet he called Munhphat (Bigmouth). Through this puppet he made many serious points, in an entertaining way. Overall they were a smash hit.

The next morning we took them to meet the people in the area near Maandal, who were troubled by the polluted water released by the processing units of the Bhilwara textile industry, which treated fabric in water with chemicals. In the evening, we had been invited by the Rajasthani film star Raj Jangid to a poetry festival at Gulabpura, where the MKSS team was to perform as they did in Maandal. By the time we reached there, some politics had been stirred up. A people's representative had complained that these people say everyone from the sarpanch to the block development officer is corrupt. They can't be allowed to perform here. Let them take back their travel expenses and leave. The MKSS refused to accept any money since they had not been allowed to perform. Instead, they found a public space in the middle of town, performed *Khajana*, sang *Chorivado* and only then did they leave. They raised one of their slogans there again and again— *nyaya samanta ho aadhar, aisa rachenge hum sansar* (Where justice and equality are the bedrock, that's the world we will build). I found this slogan attractive, and was impressed by the collective's fearlessness, determination and selflessness.

I thought to myself, one day I will find an opportunity to work with these people.

And this opportunity did come quite soon. The government of Rajasthan was conducting a social audit of the panchayats in which the largest amount of money had been spent on development. In Maandal, the audit was conducted in Bagaur panchayat. During this process I came to know the MKSS quite well. Later, social audits were conducted in some villages of Rajsamand—Lasani, Baghana, Farara and Jhalon ki Madar—and in order to cover these, I travelled with them. That is when I realised how close to the ground these people are. They act as they speak. They honestly want to bring about social transformation, and they try to live by their expressed ideals. No question of untouchability or caste discrimination among them. They did talk a bit about Gandhi, but were hardcore 'comrades', really. They also talked about Ambedkar and Periyar, Phule and Kabir—very cool people. They were using the idea of the right to information to demand transparency about the money spent by authorities in the name of the people.

I met Aruna Roy several times in this period. I also conducted a two-hour interview with her. She told me her father had been in the movement with Periyar, and that K.R. Narayanan and her father had been close. I asked her, how long should reservations continue. Her reply was—as long as discrimination, oppression and inequality continue. I was very impressed by her clarity on this matter.

I had developed a friendship with the MKSS by now. My mind was being drawn away from journalism to activism. I began to wonder, can I consider my responsibilities fulfilled by merely writing, do I demonstrate what I write, do I live by the principles I preach? Not so far, I felt. Along with covering the dharnas, I began participating in them as well, joining in the inspiring slogans. Soon, I had emerged from the mere pen-pushing of journalism, my fingers tightening into a fist, joining other fists waving in the air, my voice strengthening that of others in the chant of *Inquilab zindabad* (Long live the revolution) and *Jai Bhim, jai jai Bhim*.

In this way, having started from the RSS I reached the MKSS, exchanged my saffron band for a multicoloured one, and from an RSS swayamsevak I became a swayamsevi, a civil society activist.

40

The saffron Taliban's massacre in Gujarat

On our return to Devdungri after the public hearings held during the government's social audit, we heard that in Godhra a train had been set on fire and sixty Ram-sevaks had died in it. Everyone was very disturbed by the incident. The MKSS immediately issued a statement condemning the act, expressing sympathy to the bereaved families, and demanding the strictest punishment for the perpetrators. I had drafted this statement and it was published in the local papers.

On the day following this incident began a targeted massacre of the Muslim minority in Gujarat, in which the Gujarat government, various organisations of the Sangh and the state administration were all involved. More than two thousand people were killed. It was not a riot, for a riot involves two sides in conflict. This was a pre-planned and systematic massacre, an attempt to wipe out an entire community. The government termed it a justifiable reaction to Godhra, and attempted in the most shameful way to normalise the bloodshed.

Questions were raised about the role of the chief minister at the time, Narendra Modi, even by prime minister Atal

Bihari Vajpayee, who made a statement that 'rajdharma', or the responsibility of the ruler, had not been upheld by Modi. The government had given people of one community full freedom to express their anger in any way they wished. From senior officers of the administration to the lowest rungs of the party cadre, everyone was involved in the violence. One of Chief Minister Modi's senior ministers, Maya Kodnani, herself participated in one of the massacres, and was sentenced to a long prison sentence in 2012 (although she was acquitted by the Gujarat High Court in 2018). Many swayamsevaks of the Sangh, activists of the BJP, constables in police stations, administrative and police officials as well as lower rungs of the administration, all participated in the violence in order to be recognised and congratulated by the leader of the state. In the dance of death that spread unchecked across the state for three days, the Gujarat of Gandhi was transformed into the Gujarat of Godse. The violent Hindu mobs had lists of Muslim homes and businesses which were systematically targeted, looted, burnt.

In a housing society of Ahmedabad, Gulberg Society, former Congress MP Ehsan Jafri was cut down and set alight by a bloodthirsty Hindu mob, despite his phone calls for help to Modi himself and to Sonia Gandhi in Delhi. It is said that the police commissioner had visited Jafri and assured him of protection, and the mob attacked soon after he left. The saffron Taliban had taken over all police stations, and every call for help to a police station resulted not in deliverance but death.

From Naroda Patiya to the smallest neighbourhoods in Gujarat, mosques and tombs were demolished or burnt to ashes. Petrol bombs were thrown into Muslim settlements by saffron Hindu terrorists, gas cylinders were exploded, innocents slaughtered with swords and knives, and burnt alive. In one place, they were pushed into a well and it was filled with mud. The highly moral, disciplined, cultured and nationalist activists of the Hindu right conducted mass rapes of women in public, sliced open the stomachs of pregnant women and, pulling out the foetus at the tip of swords, swung them in the air before cutting them to pieces. The violence was frightful, indescribable. The country was horrified by these reports and deeply ashamed. The very foundation of the nation was shaken. The cruellest and most tyrannical rulers came to mind, from the ones India had known, to Hitler.

The Concerned Citizens Tribunal organised public hearings all over Gujarat and I participated in these, travelling all over the state, meeting the affected people; I visited relief camps at Shah Alam and Ramrahim Nagar.

I met and spoke to Hindus, Dalits, Muslims and Adivasis, trying to understand the terrifying situation there. The most pitiful condition was that of the Gujarati Muslims. Much of the violence had been conducted by Dalits and Adivasis, and many of them had also been killed by police bullets, as well as in the general violence. The game plan of the right-wing forces was successful. Muslims, Adivasis and Dalits died fighting each other. Thousands of Muslims were killed in the violence, and hundreds of Dalits and Adivasis died in police firing, while those who instigated the violence remained safe. Even today, these groups are set upon each other by the same forces, although they live in the same hellish circumstances, cheek by jowl with each other.

Both groups live under a cloud of suspicion—the capability of one is constantly doubted; of the other, its patriotism. Both are deeply unhappy, but those who manage religion like a business are successful in getting the poor of one community to attack the other as their enemy. Dalits attempt to prove themselves pure Hindus by taking a leading part in riots and violence against Muslims. How to make them understand that this religious minority they attack, are largely from their own community, Dalits who converted out of Hinduism, seeking equality? How to make them see that it is their own blood they shed when they kill the other, and the instigators enjoy the show? Have leaders of the VHP or Bajrang Dal or RSS ever lost their lives in a riot? Even at Ayodhya, why is it that the majority who get killed are Dalits and other Backward Castes?

The office bearers of the organisations affiliated to the Sangh, who are respected and famous, are all savarna Hindus while those who die in riots fomented by them are all Dalits and Backward Castes. The Bania seth sits comfortably in his shop, the Brahmin pandit holds forth on spirituality in the temple, while those who are pushed out to die are Dalits and Adivasis and Backward Castes. If they cannot understand this simple fact, how foolish are they?

On returning from Gujarat, I wrote an editorial in *Diamond India*, "Talibani Hindus, listen!" The issue was focused on Gujarat, from Godhra to the widespread massacres in the state. I demanded of the rulers, how was it that those of their political ideology, under their protection, had perpetrated acts never before imagined. I said, 'Even Kansa, who knew that the eighth child of his sister Devaki would kill him, did not tear open her womb, and yet, those who chant Jai Shri Krishna day and night, carried out atrocities that even Kansa would not dream of. Innocents were burnt alive, women gang raped in public, in front of crowds—this is their Hinduism?'

I went on to say that at no time had Hinduism ever been tolerant, egalitarian and non-violent, especially as far as Dalits and Shudras were concerned. No Dalit fears a bomb-hurling Taliban terrorist as much as they fear the terror of savarna Hindus. Legends and stories from the Puranas testify to the deep rooted and ancient violence in Hindu society towards Dalits, Shudras, Adivasis and women—from the killing of the Shudra sage Shambuka, to the brilliant student Ekalavya being tricked into offering his thumb as a gift to his teacher; to the rape of countless women by the devas, gods. The Hindutva heroes of today are merely following in these footsteps.

I wrote that every Dalit and Adivasi who has suffered casteist insult and untouchability sees casteist Hindus as the Taliban, as cruel oppressors. Far more painful and unbearable than bullets and bombs is the question, what is your caste, and the sudden change of behaviour upon learning it. This has to be *experienced* to be understood. Hearing or reading about it means nothing.

The Sanghis were enraged by the label of Hindu Taliban. I started getting threatening messages about teaching me a lesson, and straightening me out. I was asked to apologise. I refused to do so. Then, things got worse. We were thrown out of our Bhilwara office. The government employees among our supporters withdrew all support. It became near impossible to publish and distribute *Diamond India*, which came close to shutting down after this issue.

My friends felt I was more interested in getting into fights than in bringing out the journal, otherwise what was the need to bring out an issue in Rajasthan on a disaster in Gujarat? They too urged me to apologise; but to accept defeat and to apologise—I couldn't imagine it. I had never learnt to bow before pressure. My parents had not taught me to put up with injustice, how could I apologise? I would rather be stamped out of existence than bow down. Apologise to these people, whose hands are drenched with the blood of innocents? These people—who launched a targetted massacre of one community, raped women, looted and plundered, demolished houses, destroyed places of worship, shaming all of humanity—and I should be the one to apologise? I was clear and had no fear in refusing point-blank to apologise to these hypocritical casteist and communal forces.

Many say I am unfair in making such allegations against a nationalist and patriotic organisation like the RSS, which has never taught hatred, never been involved in any violence. No shakha of the Sangh criticises other religions, they say. Such people are either blind supporters of the Sangh or actively anti-Dalit and Muslim. From my own experience I can tell you quite unequivocally that the Sangh not only promotes enmity with the Other but even gives training in deadly weapons. Of course, these activities are not carried out publicly in the daily shakhas, but on other occasions like training camps and so on.

In the shakhas, training in the use of lathis is openly conducted, while in the OTCs, Officer Training Camps, in the first, second and third year, there is training with knives, swords and pistols in the name of self-defence. At the time of the Ayodhya movement, before karseva began, Lalbaba Premdas-ji Maharaj conducted training in making petrol bombs and Molotov cocktails in the backyard of his ashram in Bhilwara's RIICO Area Phase 3. I was there and received this training, which was meant to come in useful in the riot situations that were expected.

The Sangh is in fact a quasi-military organisation, which promotes the arming and militarising of the Hindu community. The government by now has proof of the nationwide violence conducted by individuals associated with the Sangh—the nation cannot forget the swayamsevaks who carried out bomb explosions in different parts of the country in 2006 in the name of Abhinav Bharat.

The hearings of the Concerned Citizens Tribunal before a panel consisting of Justice Hosbet Suresh, Justice P.B. Sawant, social activists Aruna Roy and Teesta Setalvad, fanned the flames of my anger. How could the administration, like Nero, calmly look the other way while the state burnt, how could any Hindu be so evil? But they did, and they were. A well-planned cleansing of one community did take place, and all evidence and witnesses were disappeared. Then, upon the wounds was applied the ointment of 'development'.

Thus emerged a 'vibrant' regime, bringing into Gujarat swarms of capitalists to sow the seeds of their greed, to be harvested in the entire country some years later. Through the work of paid trolls in social media, and corporate-controlled print and electronic media, the director of the genocide now helms the nation. Blood-drenched hands hold on to the parapet of Red Fort as we are harangued on 15 August, and the merchants of death, now our future, talk about peace, compromise, co-existence, and brotherhood. The hero of the Kaliyuga has set out from Gandhinagar and ensconced himself in Raisina Hill in Lutyens' Delhi—who can stop Delhi from becoming Gujarat?

War cries rend the air. The times are cruel. Waiting quietly for something to happen, remaining neutral and carrying on with one's life—these are not options. This is the time when our beliefs and our behaviour will be severely tested, and if we do not emerge as true and steadfast, history will never forgive us.

41

This is Hareshbhai Bhatt speaking

For a very long time after I returned from Gujarat, the stories I had heard of the massacres and its fearsome events and sights lingered with me. My mind cried out in disbelief—how can people be so cruel, cut down other humans in the name of religion. Meanwhile, threats had started, that Rajasthan would become the next Gujarat. Leaders of the VHP, Ashok Singhal and Praveen Togadia, and Hareshbhai Bhatt, Bajrang Dal national co-convenor during the Gujarat massacre, were openly making such announcements.

On 18 April 2003, we launched a cycle rally for peace against the Gujarat massacre, and collected signatures from hundreds of people along our route—from Devdungri village in Bhim tehsil of Rajsamand district to Devgarh and Kareda villages which we covered in fifteen days. We also printed some pamphlets, painted slogans on walls, and tried our best to raise people's consciousness. Meanwhile the RSS was conducting ceremonies of trishul deeksha all over Rajasthan, in which participants were ceremoniously presented with the trishul or trident, sharp edged and capable of being used as a weapon. Young Hindu men between the ages of fifteen and twenty-five were essentially being trained to take part in violent attacks through these ceremonies. Speeches spewing poison, incitement to bloodshed, these were the order of the day.

Haresh Bhatt in Bhilwara, Praveen Togadia in Rajsamand; and in Bhim, Kaluram Sankhla of the Shiv Sena Commando Force, all of them were whipping up a frenzy against Muslims. At that time one of my articles titled "This is Hareshbhai Bhatt speaking", was published by Shri Prakash Sharma in *Rajdrishti*. It was explicitly about the rise of Hindu extremism and its dangers. I was getting more and more enraged by the Sangh affiliates, and kept a close watch on all their activities. I documented the gatherings of the VHP and Bajrang Dal, whenever possible I also made recordings.

We attended the public speeches of Praveen Togadia in different places, recorded them and sent these recordings to the state government demanding his arrest. We did the same with Kaluram Sankhla who was in Bhim, inciting violence against Muslims. Here he openly declared that Muslims should be taught a lesson, and distributed swords. Our comrade activist Kheemaram Kataria played a fearless role in documenting this. On the basis of all this evidence, we later lodged a case against Kaluram Sankhla.

This hero of the stage, with his empty boasts and bluster, immediately caved in. He fled from Bhim, but was caught by the police and arrested, and we no longer had to hear his poisonous words. Praveen Togadia and Hareshbhai

Bhatt continued to speak in public meetings, hold trishul deekshas, say the most vicious things, incite violence, but the administration remained a mute spectator. Even in the administration, beneath their trousers many wore Sanghi shorts, not visible in public. You will find such secret Sanghis everywhere. The RSS has systematically planted its people in every field—media, education, politics, the administration. This is how Brahminism has succeeded in its agenda for centuries, by quietly infiltrating every space.

Dr Praveen Togadia's poisonous speeches are still a source of tension today. During the Gujarat violence, Togadia's role in fomenting violence against Muslims was so striking that Medico Friend Circle, an association of doctors, made the demand that his medical degree be revoked. They argued that Dr Togadia's activities came under misconduct as defined by the Indian Medical Council, and also were punishable under Sections 151 (A) and 153 (B) of the Indian Penal Code.

Medico Friend Circle claimed that when Gujarat was burning, and wounded and dying people being brought to hospitals in large numbers, Togadia assembled doctors in his clinic, and encouraged them to stay away from work, thus keeping them from hospitals where they were sorely needed by Muslim patients.

On 14 December 2002, he said at a press conference, 'Madarsas have become laboratories of terrorism, where students are taught to kill non-Muslims. Why should we not establish our own laboratories? We will transform the whole country into a laboratory.' Rajasthan was of course already a laboratory of this kind, with trishul deeksha and targeting of minorities.

In his speeches Dr Togadia mocked secularism as enshrined in the Constitution. He labelled secular people as donkeys and called them by other such insulting names. He said there were three kinds of Taliban in the country. First, the jihadi Taliban, who wore the long kurtas of big brother and short pyjamas of little brother (the dress of North Indian Muslims); second, the political Taliban, who for the sake of votes appeased Muslims and were willing to live as their slaves; and third, the secular Taliban who, if you placed a cow and a donkey in front of them, would worship the donkey. Togadia used to give the rousing call to uproot and throw out all these Talibans from the country.

Rajasthan was in a state of growing tension.

We placed before Ashok Gehlot's government all the evidence we had, and asked him to ban trishul deeksha and arrest Togadia. Pressure mounted on the government from all those who wanted peace and harmony. Finally, the government plucked up the courage to arrest Togadia from Ajmer where a trishul deeksha was going on.

The Togadia who roared like a lion from the stage was a very different person in police custody. Journalists present there said that all his bluster was gone, his poisonous tongue was stilled, and there were tears in his eyes. Nobody becomes brave by wearing khaki shorts and a black cap, wielding a lathi, and inflaming crowds from a stage. Courage does not come from arms, nor from the RSS uniform, nor from screaming *har har Mahadev* and *jaykaara Bajrangi* at the top of one's lungs. Anybody can be brave in a mob, like the stray dog of the locality that swaggers through its neighbourhood like a lion. But we know what cowards they are, heroes full of hollow bluster. I have seen with my own eyes how they run away from danger, tails between their legs. If the martial communities of Dalits and Adivasis were not with them, they would have run away from the country long ago. It's just an army of cowards. In any case, religious fundamentalists all over the world are bravest in mobs, and totally craven as individuals. They become heroes by attacking the weaker sections and minorities.

Kaluram Sankhla, Togadia and others like them all reached jail because of our tireless efforts. They did make bail afterwards; however, they remained quiet for some time. Only recently have they recovered the use of their tongues. And it was not only through these negative tactics that we countered the religious right-wing, we also tried to build positive alternatives, to distribute flowers of love rather than trishuls. The chairperson of the Rashtriya Sadbhavna Parishad (National Council for Communal Solidarity), the actor Raj Jangid, played a key role in this process. We took part in a padayatra, a long march that began on Ambedkar Jayanti, 14 April 2004 in Bhilwara and culminated on Labour Day, 1 May, in Bhim tehsil. In this march for the right to work, launched by the MKSS, we raised a slogan—'Not the sword, not the trishul, we want the right to live, the right to work'.

During this period the RSS and VHP folk were very angry with me. There would be open arguments, sometimes even some pushing around, although no serious physical attack. We remained steadfast in our protests until 8 April 2003, when trishul deeksha was banned in Rajasthan. We kept up the struggle until the hateful issues of swords and tridents were replaced by the issue of the right to work, which ultimately resulted in the National Rural Employment Guarantee Act.

42

Adivasis and Dalits in trishuliya Hindu Rashtra

At the height of the trishul deeksha period, I was told by Mukesh Bhargava, a top leader of the Bajrang Dal in Maandal, that an incident of blatant caste discrimination had taken place during trishul deeksha there. The ceremony was happening at the Shiv temple, Neelkanth Mahadev Mandir near the Maandal bus stand, where the procession of triumph, the shobhayatra, of young Hindu men had arrived. Each person ceremonially poured holy water on the shivlinga, and was presented with a trident.

Suddenly there was a commotion. Three young men were prevented by the pujari and others from entering the temple. They were Dalits, Valmikis. They were given trishuls but not permitted to enter the temple to perform the ritual pouring of the water, the jalabhishek. None of the VHP, Bajrang Dal and Sangh activists present tried to prevent this from happening. Mukesh Bhargava was deeply shocked by this, and he left the Bajrang Dal in protest. Although not a Dalit himself, he was horrified by the treatment meted out to fellow activists whom he had proudly addressed as Hindu brothers, and this incident led him to abandon altogether the ideology of the Sangh.

Bhargava later joined us in our struggle against communalism and our efforts to promote solidarity and goodwill.

In the light of this incident, I started challenging the organisations of the Sangh in my writings, demanding to know what their plans were for Dalits and Adivasis in their trident-equipped Hindu Rashtra to come, when already they were showing such disdain towards us. Will we be used only to carry out violence? To die and to kill in riots? Of what use were lathis and trishuls to us in this nuclear age? When their own children study in English medium convent schools, why give us the slogan of Hindi–Hindu–Hindustan? Humanity has reached the moon and circled Mars, while in their shakhas they still teach puranik mythology? I asked the Sangh why, in this age of science, they want to promote primitive weaponry like the trishul and a primitive Taliban mentality.

Of course there was no way the Sangh would answer these questions. Nor did they really have an answer to my question about the role envisaged for Dalits and Adivasis in their so-called Hindu Rashtra.

I studied the national meeting of the RSS held in Nagpur on 7, 8 and 9 March 2003, in which a thirty-six-member Akhil Bharatiya Pratinidhi Sabha (All India Representatives' Assembly) had been formed. This is the Sangh's national working committee. The Sangh that cried itself hoarse about social harmony had handed over the reins of the future Hindu Rashtra, through its national working committee of thirty-six members, to twenty-six Brahmins, five Vaishyas, three Kshatriyas and two Backward Castes (Shudras). Not a single

Dalit or Adivasi. It is very clear what the participation of Dalits and Adivasis will be in their Hindu Rashtra. Better than this is secular India, in which Adivasis and Dalits at least have 7.5 and 15 per cent reservations. Why should we Dalits participate in a Hindu Rashtra which has no place or role for us? Instead of the fraudulent slogan of *Hindu–Hindu bhai bhai,* the Sangh and its affiliates should place before the nation the facts about how many swayamsevaks and how many pracharaks, how many members of their national working committee today, are Dalits and Adivasis. If the answer is in the negative, it only proves that they still practise untouchability, and merely want to use us as unpaid labour, as they did in their agricultural fields for generations. Not as human beings equal to themselves.

I also want to ask those Dalits and Adivasis who wear the ganvesh, the RSS uniform, so proudly, and who work so hard to prove themselves dutiful swayamsevaks—in its ninety-plus years of existence, has the RSS launched a single struggle against caste and untouchability? Why has the Sangh never raised the issue of ending caste altogether? Dalits wage daily struggles for dignity, from the right to enter temples and perform yagnas, to ride a ceremonial horse to their wedding, or simply to sit quietly on a charpoy outside their own home—where is the Sangh during these struggles, in what little chicken coop does it hide itself?

Why has the practice not been ended, at pilgrimage spots from the Ganga to Pushkar, of separate ghats for separate castes to bathe? Of separate cremation grounds in every village for every caste? These Sanghis who launch movements for cow protection, and who worship rats, bulls, snakes and the like, have they once thought of Dalits who are human like themselves, about their struggle for equality? Never. And till today they stand shamelessly for the preservation of the caste system. They oppose reservation in jobs, in promotions, and want to end the SC/ST Prevention of Atrocities Act. This Sangh and the Hindu Rashtra it builds—how can there be any place for Dalits and Adivasis in it?

43

Animals, Dalits and the Chakwara pond

In Dudu, an area close to Jaipur, the capital of Rajasthan, is a village, Chakwara. Babulal Bairwa, a resident of Chakwara, was a long-time VHP member who had also participated in karseva. Disillusioned by the Sangh, he became inspired by Ambedkar's thought. Let me tell you about the incident that played an important role in opening his eyes and those of other Dalit villagers. What happened was that in the pond in Chakwara, in which all sorts of animals bathed—cows, dogs, pigs, cats, goats, buffaloes—Babulal had also dared to take a dip. He thought, I'm an activist of the VHP, a dedicated karsevak who was ready to give his life for the Ram temple. He had travelled to Ayodhya with the people of this very village. And anyway, all Hindus are equal. Well, all his illusions were laid to rest in December 2001 when the savarna Hindus of the village slapped a fine of 51,000 rupees on him for having dared, as a Dalit, to bathe in a public pond.

Babulal protested this illegal and unjust decision, pointing out that this was a common pond for the whole village, that even animals bathed in it, but not a single Hindutvavaadi organisation took this up. Exhausted, Babulal approached the

Centre for Dalit Rights in Jaipur. The issue was then taken up by human rights and Dalit rights groups and the battle to get justice for Babulal began in earnest.

Some five hundred people from all over the country launched a solidarity rally for the right of the Dalits of Chakwara to bathe in the public pond. I too was part of this rally held on 21 September 2002. The terror the Hindu Taliban is capable of unleashing was very evident that day. About forty thousand aggressive Hindus armed with lathis and other weapons advanced upon the unarmed and peaceful Dalit rally, roaring *Jai Shri Ram* and *Kalyan Dhani ki jai*. Their intention was clear. Only the police stood between the two unequal parties, as we were stopped at Madhorajpura.

Realising the seriousness of the situation, the Dalits decided to end their rally. Enraged that they could not fulfil their purpose, the maddened Hindutva mob turned on the administration and police, not sparing even senior officers, who had to run for their lives. A lathi charge and police firing followed and over a hundred people were injured.

The Dalit sadbhavna rally was a failure.

In this entire process, not one word of support for Dalits issued from the RSS. Rather, the Sangh declared the Dalit rally as a conspiracy hatched by foreigners to divide Hindu society. The mob that came to attack the Dalit rally was led by various village-level activists of the Sangh and its affiliates. It was evident that the move to defeat the Dalit struggle for justice had the full backing of the Sangh. The Manuvaadis succeeded in defeating the forces for humanity. So, not only was Babulal

Bairwa not accepted as a Hindu, he was not even recognised as a human being; his status was deemed to be beneath even animals.

The practice of seeing some humans as less than animals is an old habit of the Sangh. A good example of this is an incident in Jhajjar, Haryana, where in the presence of the police, five Dalits were burnt alive on the suspicion of cow slaughter in 2002. The Dalits were actually skinning a dead cow, which is an occupation their caste practices. There was uproar against this incident all over the country, but the response of the national general secretary of the VHP, Acharya Giriraj Kishore, was telling. He declared openly that the life of one cow is more valuable than the lives of five Dalits.

That's how much they value Dalit lives. They can drink the urine of a cow, which they consider holy, but won't even touch water offered by a Dalit. Their pet dogs and cats eat with them, sleep on the same beds as they, travel in their air-conditioned cars with them, but let alone sitting with Dalits, they will not permit even the shadow of a Dalit to fall on them. What kind of religion is this, in which those who create dirt are respected and those who clean dirt are considered inferior? Unproductive people who merely chant from almanacs and old tomes, who sit in their shops and cheat their customers and lie and lie, they are considered superior, when in thought, word and deed, they are inferior, living off the labour of others. A religion that respects not hard work but idleness. A religion based on lies and deception, which exploits women, the poor, Dalits, Adivasis.

Every day, women are insulted, oppressed; they are married off against their will, and every day, despite their not wanting it, they must offer themselves to the so-called manly needs of their husbands, which is limited to the ejaculation of semen. They are restricted in every way, punished for the smallest infringement of rules, and all the while this religion chants 'Where women are worshipped, there the gods reside' (*yatra naryastu pujyante ramante tatra devata*). Is this a religion at all, or an unjust system for the exploitation of the weaker sections of society? To call this deeply iniquitous arrangement a religion is to insult actual religions and spirituality as a whole.

Thinking about this, I am often reminded of Dr Ambedkar's words of warning to the Dalits of India: 'If Hindu Raj does become a fact, it will, no doubt be the greatest calamity for this country. No matter what the Hindus say, Hinduism is a menace to liberty, equality and fraternity. It is incompatible with democracy. Hindu Raj must be prevented at any cost.... Are not the millions of Shudras and non-Brahmins, or millions of the Untouchables, suffering the worst consequences of the undemocratic character of Hindu society?'

For Dr Ambedkar, a Hindu nation meant a nation where the savarnas would prevail over Dalits, Shudras and women.

44

The approaching footsteps of fascism

From March 2005, Bhilwara smouldered in the fires of communalism set by the trishul deeksha programmes started by the VHP in a systematic way after the violence in Gujarat. In 2002, the BJP won the assembly election and chief minister Vasundhara Raje Scindia lifted the Congress ban on trishul distribution. Businesses and institutions belonging to minority communities were targeted in different places. In Kota, a book called *Haqeeqat* (Reality) started the process of tarnishing the work of a school run by Emmanuel International Mission, founded in 1960, and a climate of tension and terror was developing against other minority institutions too. In February, the school was falsely accused of conversions and a schoolbus was attacked by Sangh activists.

On 1 March 2005, just seven kilometres from my home, in Karjalia village, Satyanarayan Sharma, the seventeen-year-old son of Ramgopal Sharma, was killed by two young Muslim men, Faroukh and Bilkis. Satyanarayan was a student of class nine in the RSS-run Adarsh Vidya Mandir and he also ran the local shakha of the Sangh. His murder aroused the anger of people, thousands were mobilised on to the streets, and Muslims were targeted violently.

This public response was managed by the leaders of the Sangh and its affiliates. At the time, the home minister of the state was a swayamsevak, Gulabchand Kataria. The situation rapidly worsened, most Muslims ran away from their homes to save themselves. Mosques and dargahs became the focus of attack. The few Muslims who stayed behind were beaten up and thrown out of the village. Not a single Muslim felt safe anywhere in the entire locality.

I personally knew the late Satyanarayan and his father from my days in the Sangh. Opposed to the Sangh as I was, I was saddened by the cruel murder. I wrote in sharp terms against the murder of the young boy, but also against the violence being carried out in his name. In the midst of this growing tension, a bloody encounter took place between the two communities, which was linked to rival criminal gangs of the region. In the shootout that took place, a Dalit boy named Raju Bairwa was killed by bullets fired by the Muslim gang. He turned out to be a top organiser of the Bajrang Dal. Although this was a gang war related to the criminal underworld, in the circumstances this incident too took a communal turn. The Bajrang Dal unleashed a violent counterattack that had the entire district up in flames.

Even as this was raging, a student of Emmanuel Mission School, Kishan Purbiya, was found hanging from a tree in his field. Again, this was taken to be a murder and the rumour spread that he had been killed by Muslims. Close to three thousand Hindus emerged on the streets and the dance of death continued for hours. When the SP of Bhilwara, Ashok Rathod, took firm steps to control the rioting, the Hindutva forces turned on him. This Scheduled Caste officer had been a thorn in the flesh of the Hindutva savarna forces, and now he was taking stern action against them. All over the district, clashes among Hindutva and Muslim groups and the police continued unchecked for a long time.

On 8 April 2005, a saffron flag was found at the door of an imambara (a building used for Eid prayers) in Maandal. The angered Muslim community took out a silent procession to register their protest. That very evening, as part of the festival of colours, Phagotsav, the idol of Vishnu as Charbhujanath, the four-armed Lord, was paraded in a ceremonial procession. At Lakhara Chowk the procession turned violent. Eleven shops and two houses belonging to Muslims were burnt, two mazars (tombs) destroyed and one mosque damaged. The police were also attacked. In the lathi charge and police firing that resulted, a Hindu youth named Kanhaiyadas Vaishnav was shot dead. The rumour was spread that pujari Kanhaiyadas had been shot by Muslims as he performed puja at the temple.

This was like adding ghee to a fire, and led to a sharp acceleration of the rampage in the whole area, with mobs organised from neighbouring villages to systematically attack Muslim businesses, places of worship and homes. Hindutva organisation leaders and Congress leaders with a leaning towards the BJP sat in the police station and directed the police towards Muslim-majority neighbourhoods where the police conducted raids. Between 9 pm and 2 am some twenty-five Muslim men were picked up by the police, thrashed mercilessly and arrested. In lockup they were abused with terms like 'Pakistani dogs' and so severely beaten that one lost his hearing and two suffered broken bones. One had his beard pulled and another was offered urine when he asked for water. During this illegal operation in Muslim neighbourhoods, the police also behaved in an uncivilised manner with Muslim women.

In this way the Muslim community of Maandal was broken—physically, socially and economically.

The happenings in Maandal were still fresh when, at five temples in Kareda village nearby, the number 786 (considered auspicious in Islam) was found written; green flags and bones of dead animals were also found. Hindus rose up violently and for seventy-two hours the market of Kareda was closed. The Sangh organisations declared these acts of sacrilege to have been carried out by the Sufi saint Sailani Sarkar who was present in Kareda at the time. They claimed that he offered refuge to Pakistani agents and criminals, that arms and weapons were stored by him, and demanded that he be removed from there. They threatened that if the administration did not do this, they would take matters into their own hands.

For many days Kareda remained tense. The police searched Sailani Sarkar's ashram thoroughly, to their heart's satisfaction, but nothing was found there. Meanwhile the acts of sacrilege at the temples were traced to Kareda resident and Shiv Sena leader Ramratan Jhanvar, alias Sintiya. When this conspiracy was exposed, Hindus were shocked, but expressed no remorse at the anti-Muslim climate that they had helped to build.

In those days in Bhilwara, idols being broken in temples, colour being thrown on mosques—these were common occurrences, and it was never clear who was responsible. The atmosphere was so poisonous that it was not possible to even be seen with a Muslim. I was deeply disturbed by all this injustice and oppression and decided to fight it openly. I wanted to expose the role of the Sangh-affiliated organisations, and along with a fact-finding team from the People's Union for Civil Liberties, produced a report, "The approaching footsteps of fascism".

No sooner was this small booklet published than all hell broke loose.

45

Sucked into my own whirlpool

The booklet thoroughly exposed Hindutva politics, its conspiracies and its role in fomenting communal violence, as well as the partisan role played by the administration and police. Naturally the booklet angered all three. Hindutva organisations declared that I was responsible for disturbing communal harmony and hurting Hindu sentiments, and filed a police complaint against me, demanding my arrest as well as a ban on the report. Without even filing an FIR the police started besieging me—the printing press was raided, copies of the booklet seized, and the printer threatened with such dire consequences that he has never spoken to me since.

Meanwhile the local leadership of the ruling BJP which included Om Bhandiya, and a journalist of vile casteist mentality, Bhairulal, along with the Bajrang Dal and the newly formed Hindu Dharma Raksha Parishad (Council for the Protection of Hindu Dharma), started threatening my comrades, saying that if they were Hindus they should abandon an anti-Hindu like me. Copies of "The approaching footsteps of fascism" were burnt in public in Maandal. I was socially and economically boycotted, and I was forbidden to step into Maandal. Under the banner of the Hindu Dharma Raksha Parishad, the same violent, riot-producing elements marched with arms to my village, to my home. There they were met with equal ferocity and fearlessness by my father and younger relatives, who had been prepared for such an attack. Of course, these cowards are never prepared for combat with equals, so they ran away, after declaring me anti-national, anti-Hindu and a tankhaiyya, one cast out of the faith.

Finally, a formal complaint was lodged against me in the Maandal police station. The state home minister gave oral orders to arrest me immediately. I was on the road between Jaipur and Bhilwara, when I received a message from a journalist friend Mahesh Agrawal, 'I have just met the SP, and the police is all set to arrest you. There is a lot of pressure from above to do so'. Immediately I contacted my people and changed my programme. I got off at Kishangarh and instead of proceeding to Bhilwara, returned to Jaipur. There I met the home secretary, P.S. Mehra, and placed my case before him. After listening to me carefully, he advised me to leave Rajasthan as the home minister was personally following my case. There were direct orders from Bharati Bhavan, the RSS headquarters, that Bhanwar Meghwanshi is to be caught and sent to jail, he is a problem.

As the situation worsened, many friends turned away from me. But when I met Aruna Roy and talked to her, she immediately spoke to Anil Vaish, the chief secretary of the state, and to human rights organisations and administrative officers in Delhi, and also started the process of moving me to

Delhi. After reaching Delhi, I was moved from place to place all over the country to keep me safe.

In Delhi, I met Kuldip Nayyar, Harsh Mander, Arundhati Roy, Bharat Dogra and Prabhash Joshi. The eminent lawyer Prashant Bhushan placed my case before the National Human Rights Commission. Aruna Roy, Mamta Jaitley and Bharat Dogra wrote articles about me in the media. Senior journalist Prabhash Joshi invited me to his home in Nirman Vihar and heard my story in full. While listening to me he kept tossing water chestnuts into his mouth, saying to me off and on, 'Eat, maharaj.' I thought this guy can't possibly help me. He is totally preoccupied with eating. But before I left his house, he called the vice president, Bhairon Singh Shekhawat, from his landline. His style was quite unique. He said, 'Bhairon Singh-ji, this is your humble servant Prabhash Joshi. Your disciple (meaning the chief minister of Rajasthan, Vasundhara Raje), is harassing our man there, please get her to see sense.' He then related to the vice president my whole story. I felt some relief and hope. The next Sunday, in his column in *Jansatta* newspaper, Prabhash Joshi wrote a piece titled "A Meghwanshi caught in a whirlpool!" (punning on my name Bhanwar).

The unity and solidarity shown by eminent journalists, litterateurs and social activists of the Hindi world, the action taken by the National Human Rights Commission in demanding explanations, and the nation-wide interest taken in my case, put the Rajasthan government on the back foot. What was astonishing though was that while rights organisations from all over the country spoke up, and the PUCL was fully involved in my assistance, not one single Dalit organisation or Dalit litterateur raised a voice in my support.

The ruling BJP realised that the attack on me had become a national issue of the right to freedom of expression and of the human rights of a Dalit journalist. The Rajasthan government was forced to declare publicly that in no police station of Rajasthan was there a formal complaint against me, and nor was there a ban on "The approaching footsteps of fascism".

So the government backed off but the social boycott of me continued. For the next three years, every time I went to Maandal, I had to first inform the police, and go there with police security. People wouldn't serve me in shops. I couldn't even get tea at the Maandal bus stop. I received threats daily. Most of my friends had ceased to be human and had become merely Hindu. Many started wearing the tilak on their foreheads. I was ostracised from society, called an enemy of Hinduism, an advocate of evil mullahs, even very close Hindu friends started avoiding me. I felt totally abandoned, even by my own shadow.

But in those terrible times some friends stood by me like rocks—Aruna Roy, Nikhil Dey, Shankar Singh from the MKSS, Raj Jangid, Tara Ahluwalia, Mahipal Vaishnav, Gangasingh Rathod, Hamid Bagwan, Yogendra Panwar, Allauddin 'Bedil', Badrilal Meghwanshi, Abid Hussain Sheikh.

I was of course fully supported by my family too. My father's gun was always loaded during that time, although it was never actually fired. Even though fully committed to non-violence, the past few years had made us feel the necessity to be equipped with arms, because our enemies did not understand the language of non-violence. They only understood the discourse of an eye for an eye. Likewise we always kept our weapons oiled and ready for these goons, and will continue to do so.

46

Suliya temple entry and Dalit consciousness

An activist of a shakha in a village somewhere told me that the shakha there had been running for fifty years continuously. Over the last seven or eight years though, the Dalits of the village, who lived in the Seva Basti settlement, had fallen prey to Dalit politics. The village had a temple to Maruti where they used to pray, content to receive prasad and observe the aarti from a distance, but now they had flung cow dung at the temple itself.

The rest of the village declared war on them, the village was split in two and tensions ran high. The activist also said to me—'Our swayamsevaks were not able to bring about a compromise because we had done no work at all in Seva Basti, and because all the swayamsevaks were non-Dalits, there was nobody the Dalits trusted.'

The question is, how did this situation arise? The organisation that was started in order to unite Hindu society on the basis of love and equality, despite fifty years of continuous work, how was it defeated by a

> movement that set out to break Hindu society, in a matter of seven or eight years?
>
> —H.V. Sheshadri, RSS leader, in the pamphlet, "Dalit andolan banam Sangh kaarya", "Dalit politics versus the work of the Sangh"

In September 2006, I had gone to meet the collector of Bhilwara, Ajitabh Sharma, on some work, and there I met a former Congress MLA of Maandal, Hafeez Mohammad. We got talking and he took me to his home, where a large number of Dalits from Suliya village had gathered. None of them had heard of me, they had come to share their woes with the former MLA; the long and short of which was that they were from a sub-caste among Scheduled Castes, the Balai, who lived in Suliya in Kareda. There, the ancestors of these Dalits, some one thousand years ago, had established a temple to Chamunda Mata, at which the pujari, priest, and those who sang at worship, were all Dalits.

In the terrible famine just before Independence, when the Dalits reached starvation point, they took their livestock and set off towards Malwa, leaving the temple in the care of a well-off Gurjar family. When they returned after a few years, they permitted the Gurjar priest to continue performing the rituals along with the Dalit pujari, and the two communities got along well. Initially there was not much income from the temple, but gradually, as more worshippers came to it, so did offerings, and the twenty-nine bighas of land belonging to the temple also appreciated in value. The Gurjar priest decided to pocket the entire income from the temple, and launched a plan to sideline the oblivious Dalits entirely. He managed to get his name as the official pujari on to documents and also took over the land, while the Dalit pujari had to be satisfied with the offerings of goat meat and bottles of alcohol at the temple.

During the Navratra festival of 2006, the Gurjars took the further step of evicting the Dalits from the temple—an easy job, as everyone from the head constable to the sub-divisional magistrate and the ministers of the state happened to be Gurjar. On the very first day of the navratras, the Gurjar priests physically attacked and pushed out the Dalit pujari, Hajari Bhopa, and other Dalits with him from the inner sanctum of the temple, and openly declared that the lowly Balais would not be permitted inside the temple henceforth.

The Dalits were unprepared for this. The temple had been built by their ancestors, and they had been priests there for centuries. They went to the Kareda police station with a complaint, but did not get a hearing. They also went to the collector and senior police officials but all of them treated it as a property dispute over land and offerings, and told them to take the matter to court. Listening to them, I wondered whether it could be dismissed merely as a property dispute—was it not really a struggle for the dignity and self-respect of an entire community? I told the Dalits there that I would come to their village with a few friends the next day and get a full sense of the circumstances. If things turned out to be as they said, I would assist them in further proceedings.

The next day I reached Suliya village with Bedil Sahab and some others and visited the temple. It had recently been renovated, during which the statues of previous Dalit priests had been removed and thrown away. It was clear the process of uprooting them and removing all signs of them from their ancestral property had begun earlier. And now, under the BJP regime, there was nobody to speak for them.

I met up with my friend, Girdhari Meghwal, and we discussed how to transform this situation into a powerful people's movement of Dalit awareness. We called a meeting of the forty Dalit families of Suliya village that night. We urged them not to see this struggle as one purely for income and land, nor to make it about belief, for I saw no point in the politics of temple entry. Indeed, personally I think it a waste of energy to fight for Dalit entry into any place of worship. The thirty-three crore gods and goddesses of Sanatana Hindu dharma have not done a thing for Dalits. Not a single deity's heart melted at our pathetic situation; not one said to his devotees, include these Dalits too, after all, they worship me as well. But whatever the differences of opinion on religion, if the fundamental rights assured by the Constitution are denied to us, then that is simply unacceptable. I did not focus on Suliya Mata, the deity, in this matter, nor the temple land nor the income from offerings. I could only see the rights assured to us by the Constitution, which needed to be won back.

I took this issue to the Central Committee of the MKSS, we met the district administration with a fact-finding report, and gave them a seven-day ultimatum. Now the ball was in their court. The report demanded that the SC/ST Prevention of Atrocities Act be invoked on this issue, and that the government take the responsibility of ensuring that Dalits could re-enter their temple with dignity.

After some internal disagreements in the MKSS on whether they should participate in a temple entry movement, finally the organisation gave us the green signal. On 18 November 2006, we called a meeting in Suliya, at which thousands of people from neighbouring villages turned up. They were addressed by Satish Kumar of the Centre for Dalit Rights, Nikhil Dey of MKSS, former BJP MP Thansingh Jatav who had left the party and become active in the PUCL, and the chairperson of SC/ST/OBC Employees' Union, Hanuman Singh Nirbhay. The meeting declared that if the administration did not ensure entry of Dalits into the temple by 12 December 2006, they would take matters into their own hands. As the news of the struggle spread, the RSS took note, the VHP jumped into the matter, and all the organisations of the Sangh stood up against the Dalits. Activists of the Sangh landed up at Kareda and started to try and defuse the growing radical consciousness of the Dalits. This episode is an excellent example of the hypocrisy of the Sangh, which talks about harmony and samrasata but works actively to prevent Dalits from fighting for their dignity.

A team from the VHP and other organisations arrived in Suliya on 23 November 2006, bringing some sold-out Dalits of their own, and met the Gurjar pujari at the temple. They tried to talk to the Dalits there, but received such an uncompromising rebuff that they had to retreat, defeated. They then went to Bhilwara and called a press conference at which they declared the struggle of the Suliya Dalits to be a conspiracy launched by multinational companies. They said that some antisocial elements were being funded by foreign forces to split Hindu society. These self-styled owners of Hinduism dismissed the struggle of the Suliya Dalits by saying that it was not an issue of discrimination against Dalits at all, as nobody but the priest can enter the inner sanctum of a temple.

Throughout this campaign, the Sangh organisations acted in an extremely duplicitous manner. On the one hand BJP, Bajrang Dal, VHP, Shiv Sena, all put forward their Dalit activists to discredit the Suliya struggle. On the other, the local BJP MLA and a cabinet minister of the BJP government, Kalulal Gurjar, organised a fraudulent temple entry on 26 November. They brought some Dalits-on-rent from outside, who were taken up to the verandah of the temple and presented before the media. These hired Dalits were then made to say that there was no discrimination against Dalits in Suliya.

On the evening before the farce of temple entry enacted by the minister, high-level talks at the Bhilwara district headquarters had broken down. To my astonishment, a senior official of the administration challenged me at this meeting to provide written proof that Dalits used to worship at the temple earlier. Without such proof, he said, they could do nothing.

In the presence of the district collector and other officials, I said to him: 'In those 'earlier' days, Dalits could not step out of their homes till the afternoon, could not study, had no rights—there was no question of their going to temples. So we don't need proof from 'earlier' days. All we need to know is that *today*, the Constitution created by Dr Ambedkar gives the right to all Dalits to enter all public places of worship, and they cannot be prevented from doing so. The 'proof' you ask for is the Constitution of India in which we believe. In what does your administration believe?'

Eventually the district administration, police and political party activists got the message loud and clear that the Dalits of Suliya were not fighting for temple entry and worship and prasad. They were fighting for equality. This fight could not be laid to rest by enacting a drama of temple entry. The next day that drama did take place, but the Dalits of Suliya did not participate in it. The official temple entry remained an empty formality. Eventually, over five thousand Dalits and Adivasi men and women entered Suliya Mata's temple despite all opposition. It was a historic victory.

I did not go into the temple and the media made much of the story that the leading activist of temple entry had himself not entered the temple. However, in the meeting that morning, I had announced that I had no intention of entering the temple, and I did not see the path of liberation for Dalits in temples and mosques.

The temple entry at Suliya was an epochal event. The campaign had gone on for three months, and the process had taught Dalits how to organise, how to conduct a struggle, and the eventual victory taught them that struggles can indeed be won.

The movement resulted also in the formation of the Dalit, Adivasi and Ghumantu Rights Campaign (DAGAR), which brought together these three communities of southern Rajasthan. The Ghumantu are a denotifed nomadic tribe. Young people of these communities built a powerful movement, which spread to Bhilwara, Rajsamand, Chittorgarh, Udaipur, Pali, Ajmer and Banswada, where the voices of the marginalised were strengthened by their intervention.

Meanwhile, the victory of the Dalits in Suliya made the minister Kalulal Gurjar and the Bhilwara superintendent of police Govind Gupta very unhappy. They could not tolerate the growing Dalit assertion, and the fact that in incident after incident Dalits were standing up against oppression, discrimination and injustice. When the balance of power in society began to falter, the Sangh and its affiliates started with their usual tactics, accusing me of conspiring with Muslims and Christians to break Hindu society. The minister and SP tried to embroil me in a false case. Two of my close associates were actually arrested on cooked-up charges and they spent a year in jail.

When I got wind of the conspiracies against me from my sources in the senior levels of the administration and intelligence agencies, I met with the courageous crusader for democratic rights, the lawyer Vivek Bhatnagar. Along with advocate Pankaj Ranka, advocate Bhatnagar filed a case on my behalf under Section 156 (3). This section of the Indian Penal Code gives the magistrate the power to direct the officer in charge of a police station to hold a proper investigation that can be monitored by the magistrate. This strategic move tied the hands of Kalulal Gurjar and SP Govind Gupta, and aborted their plan to throw me into prison to rot.

The matter came to be investigated by the CID and CBI. I had two powerful witnesses in Balulal and Girdhari. The matter went on and on. Eventually the SP was transferred and the minister sent back home by the people.

The false cases registered against me as part of the political conspiracy were closed. My battle however carries on till today. After Suliya, in Bhairukheda village, after a five-year battle, Ganpat Bareth and his family regained entry into the village, and the Bhil pujaris driven out of Atlaji Mandir were reinstated. During that difficult period, eleven Dalits were killed by savarna Hindus in Bhilwara, hundreds of people were wounded in different violent incidents and atrocities against Dalits were committed in some six-hundred places. Using news reports of three of these years, a detailed fact-sheet was prepared by Sowmya Sivakumar and Eric Kerbart for the Research for People group, which was a striking illustration of how skilfully facts and the truth can be presented.

DAGAR, the caravan that set out in 2006, has still not reached its destination. Thousands of Dalit youth have joined the organisation, and at one call, massive gatherings can materialise. Dalit consciousness has set foot on a new track. Of course, as Dalits become more assertive, Sanghi conspiracies to subvert this assertion also keep pace. But because our numbers grew so massively, organisations of the Sangh now hesitated to attack us physically, and launched more subtle measures, as I was about to learn.

I was soon to be approached by Sanghi hunters with well-baited traps, about which more later.

47

Love Jihad v. *dhai aakhar prem ka*

From my days in the shakhas, I had often heard that one of the main ambitions of Muslim men was to have sex with a Hindu woman at least once in their lives. They believe it brings them savab, or reward in heaven. This longing is what drives them.

It was difficult to believe this at first, but as it was repeated again and again, I began to accept it as truth. They would say, look at Muslim students in school or college, they are less interested in studies and more in attracting Hindu girls. Gradually it appeared to me to be true, that Muslim boys were indeed only interested in getting Hindu girls to fall in love with them.

My entire outlook changed. I felt as if every Muslim youth was engaged in this project. The term 'love jihad' had not come into existence then, but the same kinds of things were said. It was said that after working in iron foundries and garages all day, these men emerged in the evening all dressed up, in search of Hindu women. They land up at our fairs, at our community dandiya dance, everywhere. It was often lamented, what do our women see in them!

A young and rising leader in those days held the view that it was because Muslim men eat meat while Hindu men are vegetarian. Non-vegetarian food increases the libido, where the sattvik vegetarian diet of Hindu men douses sexual desire. One time a Sanghi lawyer declared, you know what, the root of their attraction is circumcision, Hindu women cannot resist this aspect of Muslim men. I didn't understand much of this at the time. Later I certainly rethought many of these beliefs, but during my childhood, the stories took deep root in my mind.

In the shakha we used to try and figure out ways of countering this campaign of Muslim men to trap Hindu women. We decided that we should encourage Hindu men to do the same with Muslim women, inspire them by saying that having sex with a Muslim woman would bring as much merit in heaven as feeding a hundred cows. We should offer formal rewards to those Hindu boys who got Muslim women to fall in love with them. This kind of crude talk occupied us entirely for a long time, and only gradually faded away.

Now that 'love jihad' is talked about so much, these old discussions come to mind. Nothing has changed, the same old third-rate views are circulating, stronger than ever, now with a shiny new name, still poisoning the air between the communities. The fruits of a long secret preparation are now in the open. 'Love jihad' was always on the agenda of the Sanghis, and now an old wound has become a suppurating sore.

If you ask me, love is a jihad in itself. Falling in love, and staying in love is nothing short of a dharmayuddha, a crusade. What is so unfortunate is that these merchants of hate want to poison love too. I hope that despite all the nonsensical talk about jihad, hearts will meet, that people will fall in love, leaping across the borders of caste and religion and community and country. That the religious right-wing will be rejected in its attempts to police love, that these walls will fall one day.

As for me, my family never gave me the chance ofbecoming a love jihadi. I was engaged the moment I was born, married as a child, and on becoming an adult I had to start living with my wife. When people get close to me, they ask, 'Have you ever fallen in love?' I answer, I married love. For twenty-seven years I have been married to Prem, her very name means love, we have been life partners. Our lives are very different. My world is that of books, hers that of farming and livestock. I sling my cloth bag on my shoulder and wander about talking of social transformation, she remains steadfast as the axis around which my home spins.

As it happens, we never fight. Unlike traditional married couples, we have never had the time to shout at each other. Never have we shown our love by saying 'I love you', nor have we ever reached the opposite point of yelling 'I hate you'. Our harmonious relationship has not needed explicit expression of feelings, and I hope it never becomes dependent on words. My life is full of love—my children Ashok, Mamta, Vimla and Lalit, my loving parents. At every step I am supported by all of them. Whatever I am today, it is thanks to my family. Had I not had such a pleasant and happy family life, I might have been engaged in anti-social, not social, work.

Although my life partner never went to school or had a formal education, her intelligence and understanding is such that our home runs like a dream; she is an amazing blend of generosity and modern thinking. Never has she doubted me or argued with me as I did the work that occupies me. She has not read any feminist literature, or been part of any feminist organisations, but she is outspoken in her feminist beliefs. Atrocities against Dalits, women being called witches and lynched—she has been at the forefront of protests and political action against these. In fact, she is the real head of our household, she gave new meaning to our lives, and with her simplicity she has built a beautiful world for us.

Of course, life is not simple, nothing is as straightforward as it might appear on the surface, there are ups and downs. It has sometimes felt as if we are life partners only in name, but the two and a half letters that Kabir says make up the word prem *(dhai aakhar prem ka)*—this love has always survived every trial. My life with Prem, my marriage to her, has taught me that at any point in life one could meet someone, at any point lose someone, one never knows. It is all a matter of fortuity. But I am grateful for the countless blessings in my life, and my heartfelt desire is that there comes a day when the words 'love' and 'life' become synonymous. Then words like 'love jihad' won't even matter.

48

The conspiracy to defeat Dalit consciousness

Many leave the RSS and remain away from it for years, but though they are not active, they act as sleeper cells. They don't oppose the Sangh and, from time to time, whenever necessary, they may be reactivated. In the Sangh's understanding, no swayamsevak ever really leaves; no swayamsevak *was* one. Once a swayamsevak, you are one for life, whether you attend shakha or not. In this sense I too was regarded as a swayamsevak, if one in the category of being 'negatively active'. Ever since the demolition of the Babri Masjid, I have been exposing the hypocrisy of the Sangh and its affiliates. Using their own weapons, I have kept fighting them. While they often attacked me with ferocity, at other times they tried to bring about a reconciliation. When I sometimes ran into my old Sanghi acquaintances, they would ask with sadness, what went wrong? How did we lose a swayamsevak like you? What are you angry about, really?

The reason for my anger has been explained many times in writing as well as in speech, as these people know very well. They kept trying for an opportunity to meet with me and counteract my anger, make it dissolve, and I never took their pretend concern seriously. I knew what the strategy was, to keep me close to themselves and slowly suffocate my voice. They are most affected by my accusations of hypocrisy regarding Hindutva, that their proclaimed ideology and their politics show far apart in the actual and inhuman treatment of Adivasis and Dalits. Whenever we raised the question of discrimination in temples and the widespread practice of untouchability in villages, the Sangh and its affiliated outfits would become defensive. At the local level, the Sangh's tame Dalits acted as a shield for the RSS, landing up wherever Dalit struggles were going on, to give casteist savarna Hindus the clean chit. Some of them are allotted this specific task by the RSS in different parts of the country. The job of such anti-Dalit Dalits is to subvert any influence of Ambedkar, Buddha, Phule or Kabir anywhere, by the invocation of puranic stories to mislead and confuse Dalits and Shudras.

The Sangh has highlighted every possible legend and myth that encourages Shudras to remain faithful and devoted servants of the caste system. From the story of Valmiki, the supposed Dalit who wrote about the glories of Ram; to Sabari who innocently tasted the berries she then fed to Ram; to Ekalavya, the archer who gave up his thumb, and with it his skill, to his Brahmin teacher Drona as guru dakshina—all of them Dalits, Shudras and Adivasis who bowed humbly before their savarna lords. For years the RSS has been distorting the history of Dalits, trying to portray them as Kshatriyas in disguise. They began with the Valmiki-isation of the mehtar or sweeper community, taught them they are direct descendants of the writer of the *Ramayana*. They opened RSS schools in their neighbourhoods. Drew the educated into their web of seductive words. The results are for all to see. The sections that Hindu society pushed to the bottom as the most inferior, treated in the most inhuman way, are now ready to sing the praises of the very system that oppresses them. They feel honoured to be recognised as the children of Valmiki himself, this is their reward.

I wonder why the descendants of the Rishi Valmiki whose hand wielded the pen to write the *Ramayana*, find their own hands adorned with brooms, and their heads with baskets of rubbish? But who can resist Sanghi propaganda? Dalit castes are being persuaded that the cause of their current pathetic situation are the Mughals, Greeks, Pathans, and Muslims; because before they entered Bharat, there were castes, but no discrimination based on caste. It was Muslim rulers who introduced these hateful practices. Hindus have nothing to do with the five-thousand-year old Brahminical and Manuvaadi varna and caste system, which has oppressed and enslaved lower castes in the most inhuman ways possible. Rather, Dalits are being taught that their ancestors are warriors who bravely fought the Mughal and other Muslim invaders, and when they lost, were made into slaves.

According to the Sangh, the root cause of caste oppression is the Muslim, not the casteist Hindu. How cunning this ruse is, Hindus get away free and clear, dumping the responsibility on others. But what can be done. The poisonous creeper of the RSS, planted in 1925, is abloom now with flowers. Such histories continue to be written. For instance, a writer beloved of the Sangh, Vijay Sonkar Shastri, wrote histories of three Dalit castes, released by Sangh chief Mohan Bhagwat. Even the titles of these books appear Manuvaadi, insulting, and intended to subvert Dalit consciousness—*Hindu Charmkar Jati*, *Hindu Khateek Jati*, and *Hindu Valmiki Jati*. The prefixing of 'Hindu' to these oppressed castes—of leather workers, butchers and cleaners—and the propagandist books that eulogise their occupations reinforce the caste ideology of Manu. It is clear that through such books, the RSS wants to free itself from any responsibility for the shameful system of caste discrimination and oppression, and pass that burden on to Muslims, thus pitting Muslims and Dalits against one another.

49

Samrasata, the Sangh's humbug

The relentless questioning of the Sangh and its affiliates regarding the place of Dalits and Adivasis, has shaken it to the core. The challenge posed by progressive and democratic thought, as well as the ideas of Buddha, Phule, Kabir, Periyar and Ambedkar, have made the Sangh very uneasy. Questions have been raised in the Sangh about equality and equal participation. The Sangh's passivity on untouchability and caste discrimination has been noticed, it is being challenged to demonstrate its commitment to ending these practices, or be held responsible for fostering them. Why has the Sangh not initiated a single movement against casteism, caste discrimination, and the oppression of Dalits and Adivasis? Does the Sangh support inter-caste marriage, and if so, how many swayamsevaks have married outside their caste? What is the Sangh's opinion on reservations for the marginalised? What about the other unspoken reservation over centuries, for those privileged by birth into specific castes? What is the programme the Sangh has outlined to end discrimination and bring about equality? Does the Sangh have any plans to amend those religious texts that speak demeaningly of Shudras and women?

Many such questions are being addressed to the Sangh.

In 2012, the Sangh decided to work seriously on these issues and try to address these questions to the extent possible. The concept of samrasata or harmony was taken up as the core belief. Although the term has an older history in the Sangh, it was given greater emphasis and taken up on a war footing. The first step was to identify all the individuals and organisations who had been raising such questions, especially the most influential faces in Dalit movements, with possible ambitions in politics. Systematically, the Sangh began to contact such people, from the local level to Delhi. Those whose desire was to become a councillor or sarpanch received the appropriate assurances; so did those who wanted to become MLAs or MPs. The sad truth is that eminent Dalits who had fought the Sangh for years were seduced by these measures and lost the sharpness of their beliefs, ending up as spokespersons for the Sangh.

The second task the Sangh took up was the rewriting of literature to do with Dalits and Backward Castes, by involving people of these communities who had worked in the Sangh and the BJP for decades. They were given the job of writing caste histories that presented Hindu texts and the Brahminical system as noble and egalitarian, placing the entire responsibility for caste-based evils on Muslim invaders, thus obviating the need to amend religious texts in any way.

The third task was to appropriate the legacy of Ambedkar

and to corrupt it. To propagate as Ambedkar's words things he had never said or to quote his words out of context, so that he could be shown as anti-Muslim and a supporter of the Hindu Rashtra. Stories circulated that were completely cooked up: something Ambedkar was reported to have said to a pracharak; Ambedkar attending an RSS meeting, accepting the saffron RSS flag as a gift—such concocted accounts were circulated to show that Ambedkar supported the Sangh and its agenda. This kind of propaganda around Ambedkar continues till today.

The fourth task was to defame progressive and left-wing organisations that worked for Dalit and Adivasi rights, by spreading rumours that they were funded by Christians abroad, and were trying to destabilise the country. The whole point was to ensure that Muslims, Christians, Dalits and Adivasis should not come together. This campaign has picked up speed since then, especially after the BJP came to power at the centre. Such organisations are being officially hounded, investigated, and their funds restricted by manipulating the Foreign Contribution Regulation Act (FCRA).

In order to achieve social harmony or samajik samrasata, the Sangh has launched a campaign for 'One temple, one cremation ground, one source of water' (*ek mandir, ek smashan, ek panghat*). If it will take everyone sitting together and eating together to make Dalits stay within the fold of Hinduism, then let's do it, seems to be the spirit of this campaign. They are also trying to look at inter-caste marriage positively, since they understand the importance of keeping Dalits and Adivasis with them. Despite making this their main agenda, their real intentions are revealed by Mohan Bhagwat's statements on reservations. Periodically Bhagwat calls for a debate on reservations, implicitly and sometimes explicitly criticising the policy, and when there is an uproar, the RSS clarifies that it is not against reservations.

As a result, once again the RSS project of samajik samrasata has been derailed. Once again Dalits, Adivasis and the Sangh are in two enemy camps.

50

The slippery paths of politics

On the one hand, then, the attempts to subvert Dalit consciousness; on the other, to appropriate Dalit heroes. In the morning prayer at shakhas, the RSS invokes Dr Ambedkar, Buddha, Kabir and Phule. It appears as if communal forces have embraced these great souls. But this is mere deceit, a trick to reverse the growth of Dalit consciousness. The Sanghis want to present themselves as having imbibed the ideals of every layer of society, and as being truly nationalist. What they really want to do, of course, is to devour every one of our heroes.

About three years ago, the RSS took a decision to seek out every individual of the Dalit and Adivasi communities who spoke up for their rights, and to win them over with awards, honours, posts, prestige.

The Sangh had come to understand that as long as Dalit and Adivasi votes went to secular parties, it was impossible for the BJP to come to power. Also that ideologically, Dalits, Adivasis and Backward Castes would never get caught in the Sanghi maze. This is why they adopted the strategy of appealing to power-hungry, self-styled leaders of Dalits in a calculated way. Following Nagpur's directions, from the village level to Delhi, they laid on blandishments. The likes of Ram Vilas Paswan and Dr Udit Raj were yoked to the plough by Rajnath Singh, while the ring on Athawale's nose was held tight by Gadkari. However critical such leaders may have been of the Sangh in the past, all their sins were forgiven, and it was the BJP's job, strictly supervised from Nagpur, to somehow bring under the umbrella of the RSS, every single leader who spoke for Dalits and Adivasis.

It was the eighth wonder of the world for me when the BJP and Sanghis reached out even to me, the most outspoken of their critics. They didn't approach me directly, but tried to tempt me through long-time associates of mine in Bhilwara. They were told that they should persuade me to enter politics actively, so that I could bring about positive transformation for a larger number of people. Thus the message reached me that some Sanghis and people from the BJP wanted to meet me in my village. I sent back the reply that I don't refuse to meet with anyone, and would be happy to meet them publicly, as long as I know the purpose behind such a meeting.

I also decided that any such meeting should not be at my home, Ambedkar Bhavan, but in Bhilwara. Finally, as my friends were very keen for it to happen, the meeting took place. Present were the district head of the BJP, Subhash Bahediya (member of parliament at the time of writing); the MLA from Bhilwara city, Vitthalshankar Awasthi; a former pracharak of the Sangh, Vinod Melana; the regional pracharak, Durgadas and some other people. At first there was no conversation about politics. After a bit of chit-chat, the senior functionary of the Sangh said to me, 'What happened with you during the Ramjanmabhoomi movement, [he meant the shameful incident of the food from my home being thrown out on the road], that is not the kind of behaviour authorised by the Sangh. It was certainly the mistake of individual swayamsevaks, and you are justified in being angry. But in that anger you have undertaken such negative activities as have greatly harmed the Sangh and Hindu society as a whole. As a result of your activism, our society has been weakened. Now we urge you to use your energies positively in the national interest. You are a popular leader of marginalised communities, and you can serve their interests better if you join hands with the Sangh and BJP. You should join the BJP as soon as possible, and we will start the work of providing you with an assured seat.'

I was totally relaxed, sat back and took a sip of tea. I was well-versed in Sanghi tactics. I had no reason to have any faith in the Sangh. Even the disguised words of apology gave me no satisfaction. For twenty years the sting of that insult had smouldered in me, it could not be erased in a moment. I just listened to them. I knew their words came from no deeper than their throats. Just as I knew I would remain true to my commitments, and my views were not going to change, I knew neither would they. They would fail in making me fall in with Hedgewar's agenda, just as I would fail in influencing them with Ambedkar's thought.

On my lips was the salutation Jai Bhim; on theirs was Ram, but they carried a concealed knife, as the saying goes. The meeting was bound to end without resolution, and it did.

I put them off at the time by saying I would consult my people and then decide. We did have an intense debate on this later, and came to the conclusion that we should stay as far away from the Sangh and its affiliates as possible or else our entire movement would be swallowed up by them.

There were many other developments behind the scenes, some leaders had their own selfish aims. The rumour was spread widely, from Bhilwara to Delhi and from Jaipur to Nagpur, that an old swayamsevak's homecoming, or gharwapsi, was imminent. Some of my enthusiastic supporters even toured a chosen Legislative Assembly constituency. Somebody met Vasundhara Raje, someone else Bhupendra Yadav. Another met a minister in Delhi, and yet another met Mukhtar Abbas Naqvi, the Muslim face of the BJP. Also Gulabchand Kataria and Arjun Meghwal. For three months it was a flurry of activity, but it was all a kind of marking time, with no progress, because both sides were bluffing.

The people who were proclaiming they would take me into the BJP were those whose politics were directly opposed to mine. Many had joined in with 'Mission 72' and signed on to end reservations for Dalits. Mission 72 refers to the 72 per cent of the population that is not covered by reservations for Dalits and Adivasis, who together get 28 per cent reservation in Rajasthan. So Mission 72 is an anti-reservation campaign. There were others whose mines had been closed by our struggles to save forests. And still others who had publicly accused me of joining forces with Muslims and Christians to destroy Hindu society. Some VHP elements who now came to meet me used to call me a Naxalite. Now I was acceptable to all of them, suddenly I was a nationalist. Those who once abused me freely could not stop praising me now. They were absolutely certain that I would finally move into the shelter of the BJP and contest elections from the Shahpura constituency in Bhilwara. For three months I travelled along the slippery paths of politics. Went to thousands of villages and placed before our people this issue. Most of them said we trust you, we know you will not take the wrong step.

In the social sector though, most were repelled by the very idea. The MKSS in particular was angry that I could even consider it. They were extremely unhappy at this apparent corrosion of their comrade's ideals. In those days my communication with them had virtually broken down. I had stopped even talking to them. Aruna Roy sent me a message that whatever decision I finally took, I should please meet her once. One night, Shankar Singh, Nikhil Dey and Parashram Banjara came home, stayed the night. It was like a family gathering. They said nothing, but their feelings were clearly evident on their faces. I had realised by then that it was time to end the farce. After all, how long would I carry on pretending to walk a path I had no intention of traversing.

Finally, on 14 April 2013, at the conclusion of the Kabir Phule Ambedkar awareness walk, at Azad Chowk in Bhilwara, in the presence of thousands of people I rejected the RSS, saying, 'I am not entering politics or contesting elections. There is no question of my ever joining a communal organisation. I will always work towards transforming society, not government.'

And thus I freed myself from the clutches of the Sangh, making them angrier than ever. They say I cheated them, which in a way is true enough. Although considering what they did to me, what I did is nothing.

51

In conclusion

Many friends were angry that I decided not to join politics, especially those who wished to see me in some sort of high post. The Sangh had managed to influence them deeply, and since they were very close to me, they proved effective as weapons for the Sangh to defame me widely.

From among the thousands who had celebrated me earlier, many began to slip away, they must have felt this man is of no use to us if he doesn't join politics. He will just wander about with a cloth bag on his shoulder. In fact he is a burden on us, with his views and his politics. Such kind of selfish elements that were anyway close to the Sangh and the BJP, were back with the enemy the moment these forces came to power in Rajasthan in 2013.

Once the BJP came to power in Rajasthan and Narendra Modi was enthroned in Delhi, the violent face of power was revealed very clearly. The Sangh–BJP combine used everyone from my neighbours to my former companions, against me and my family. Members of my family faced life-threatening physical attacks, false cases were slapped on me, cooked up complaints led to probes. The police, CID, CBI, IB, all carried out multiple investigations. These forms of extreme harassment carry on till today. The Sangh outfits also tried to defame me with the MKSS, by sending some letters, which too were investigated. I was a full-time worker of the MKSS from February 2012 to July 2015. Some anonymous letters accused me of embezzlement of funds, and that I had built a house, acquired a Bolero jeep and lived an un-Gandhian life that did not behove a civil society activist. A seven-member committee enquired into these allegations and found them baseless and motivated. The trauma and agony this caused left me alienated even from the civil society space, and I became truly independent. Thus, Vasundhara Raje's and Modi's reign have been marked for me by complaints, cases, accusations, investigations, clarifications—and it carries on relentlessly, but I refuse to accept defeat.

I know the empire of the Sangh and the BJP stretches from my village to Delhi, but I try to stand by my principles in the same way as I always have. I have spoken out fearlessly against every incident of violence against Dalits or minorities, and I intend to continue doing so. I know that the Sangh and various outfits affiliated have moved now from abuse to bullets (from gaalis to golis), and that many rationalists and progressive and anti-communal people have been shot dead, many more are in their line of sight.

Nevertheless I will speak, I will write, and I will always stand up, speak out, and fight the battle against injustice, oppression, exploitation and inequality.

Inquilab zindabad—Long live the revolution!

Bhanwar Meghwanshi was born in 1975, the year of the Emergency, into a Kabirpanthi weaver family in Sirdiyas village in Rajasthan. Thinking it was fun and games, he joined the Rashtriya Swayamsevak Sangh during his schooldays and became a zealot. After leaving the RSS, he taught in a government school for two years. Since 2001 he has been an activist and a journalist chronicling the Dalit movement. He's been associated with the Mazdoor Kisan Shakti Sangathan and People's Union for Civil Liberties. He edits the e-zine shunyakal.com and is invited by various peoples' movements to conduct workshops, talks and cadre camps. He currently divides his time between overseeing the Ambedkar Bhavan in Sirdiyas and his political work that takes him across the country.

Nivedita Menon, professor of political thought at Jawaharlal Nehru University, New Delhi, is the author of *Seeing like a Feminist* (2012). Active in democratic politics in India, she founded the collective blog, kafila.online. She has translated fiction and non-fiction from Hindi and Malayalam into English and from Malayalam into Hindi. She received the 1994 A.K. Ramanujan Award for translation instituted by Katha. In 2016, she translated Geetanjali Shree's Hindi novel, *Khali Jagah*, as *The Empty Space.*